The
Fisher
Queen

The Fisher Queen

A deckhand's tales of the BC coast

Sylvia Taylor

VICTORIA · VANCOUVER · CALGARY

Heritage House Publishing Company Ltd.
heritagehouse.ca

LIBRARY AND ARCHIVES CANADA CATALOGUING IN PUBLICATION
Taylor, Sylvia, 1954–
The fisher queen: a deckhand's tales of the BC coast / Sylvia Taylor.

Issued also in electronic format.
ISBN 978-1-927051-53-5

1. Taylor, Sylvia, 1957–. 2. Women merchant mariners—British Columbia—Pacific Coast—Biography. 3. Authors, Canadian (English)—Biography. 4. Fishers—British Columbia—Pacific Coast. 5. Fisheries—British Columbia—Pacific Coast. 6. Pacific Coast (B.C.)—Biography. I. Title.

HD6073.F672C3 2012   331.4'8238282   C2012-903831-8

Edited by Barbara Stewart
Proofread by Lana Okerlund
Cover design by Ruth Linka
Interior design by Sandra Baskett
Cover photo: Trolling the Southeast Corner fishing grounds outside Ucluelet, on the west coast of Vancouver Island (Paul Taylor).
Frontispiece photo: A 40-foot ladder for the sake of a skinny little spring salmon or two, Neptune Packers Ltd., Ucluelet (Paul Taylor)
Marine charts reproduced with the permission of Canadian Hydrographic Service. *These charts are not to be used for navigation.*

The interior of this book was produced on 100% post-consumer recycled paper, processed chlorine free and printed with vegetable-based inks.

Heritage House acknowledges the financial support for its publishing program from the Government of Canada through the Canada Book Fund (CBF), Canada Council for the Arts and the province of British Columbia through the British Columbia Arts Council and the Book Publishing Tax Credit.

 Canadian Heritage Patrimoine canadien   The Canada Council for the Arts | Le Conseil des Arts du Canada    BRITISH COLUMBIA ARTS COUNCIL

16 15 14 13 12 1 2 3 4 5
Printed in Canada

For my father, Laimon Cirulis,
whose greatest pride was becoming
a Canadian and building a life for his family in
what he called the "God's Country" of British Columbia

Acknowledgements

They say it takes a village to raise a child; the same can be said of a book. Deepest love and gratitude to all the villagers who nurtured and guided me and *The Fisher Queen* through this incredible voyage and brought us safely home. All the open hearts in all the places, that listened and loved the stories.

This book of the watery Northwest was born in the sizzling Southwest desert, where I went to write a historical novel of the Pacific Northwest and came home with 15 stories that grew into a chronicle of a way of life lost to us, and the last vestiges of Canada's Wild West. To the First Nations people of the Pacific Northwest who have revered the salmon and its habitat for 10,000 years, and all the fishers everywhere who risk life and limb to feed the world, all the Salty Dogs who are still with us and those who forever troll the celestial fishing grounds: may you always have a smiley on every hook.

To Heritage House Publishing and its phenomenal crew of literary pilots and navigators, especially managing editor Vivian Sinclair and editor Barbara Stewart, whose steady hands at the tiller, unerring eye on the compass and deep belief in the work moved us always towards excellence and authenticity.

Infinite thanks to all the writer-folks who tirelessly encouraged, supported, nagged and finally stood cheering on the dock to welcome

The Fisher Queen home: agent-extraordinaire Donald Maas and his wonder-editor wife, Lisa Rector Maas, for lovingly reminding me to "just write the damn book"; Esther Sarlo, whose insightful preliminary edits, passionate belief and endless cheerleading kept me afloat along with my brilliant writer-group pals, Pamela Tarlow-Calder, Bill Chalmers, Cathleen Chance Vecchiato, Tony Ollivier, Bill Burns, Ed Griffin, Sarah King, Rupert Macnee and world adventurer Anthony Dalton, who led me and my "darn good story" to Heritage House.

To wise and loving Richard Tarnoff who saw the light inside me then and now and served as technical advisor on all the fishing-related stuff, and always had my best interests at heart. Tom and Annette Phillips, Jane and Wayne Garrison, and the writing communities of Arizona who adopted me as their own and rode herd on me for the last six years. The Barn Boys, my first "guy test group," who laughed and wept their way through the stories, in a manly way, of course. To Paul, who was the catalyst of that grand adventure and stepped up 27 years later to make it right.

To Beenie and Etta, my dear ol' BFFs, who always loved and believed in me even when I didn't.

To Anastasia, who passed the writer gene on to me, and my brother, Martin, who always knew it was there. To Mum, who helped set me on the path by retrieving my crumpled poem from my bedroom floor when I was 12 and sending it to a CBC poetry competition so I could win. And to Dad, who always wanted this for me.

Contents

Jostling cheek to jowl for a spot on the wharf at the government floats in the inner harbour at Ucluelet. PAUL TAYLOR

The Legend of Sisiutl

A Story of the First Nations of the Pacific Northwest

From the depths of the sea between the mountains, from the doorways of the Supernaturals he fiercely guards, the great serpent comes.

Wings of Thunderbird, twin heads of Wolf, silver sides of Salmon, forked tongue of Snake, fierce heart of Dragon, earth wisdom of Bear. Travelling in seas and rain and blood and tears, he transforms himself, for he is the Shape Shifter, the Soul Searcher, the Truth Seeker.

He comes to judge all Humankind. He comes to judge your courage, your heart, your soul, your spirit. He finds you in your deepest, darkest fear. He comes to you in your life-changing times.

And when his fearsome head rises from the waters and his gaze burns deep into your heart and soul, you must stand your ground and face your horror, face your fear. And when his second, more fearsome head rises from the waters to steal your soul, each face will see the other, your True Self reflected in them.

The ones who cannot control their fear, whose hearts are filled with darkness, who cannot hold their Truth, are devoured or turned to stone as they run from him.

Those who hold Truth and Courage, who stand in their authentic selves, he blesses with wisdom and magic and bids them return to their lives as Chosen Ones, to be leaders and beacons for others.

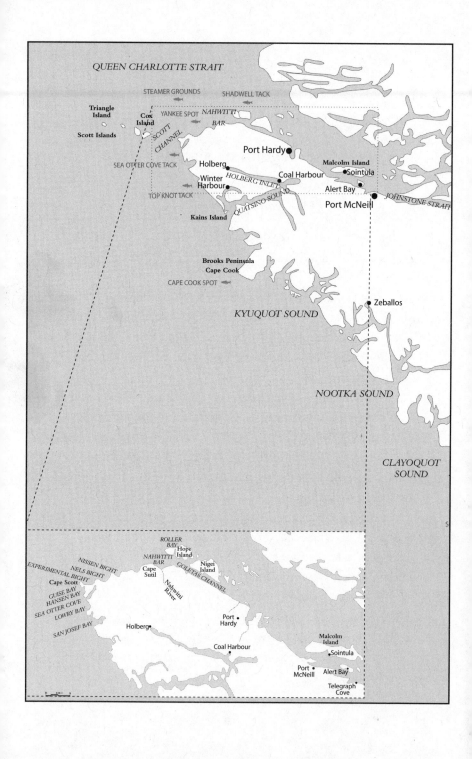

QUEEN CHARLOTTE STRAIT

STEAMER GROUNDS   SHADWELL TACK

Triangle Island   Cox Island   YANKEE SPOT   *NAHWITTI*
                                              BAR
Scott Islands   SCOTT
                                   CHANNEL

SEA OTTER COVE TACK   Holberg   *Malcolm Island*
                              HOLBERG INLET   Coal Harbour   Sointula
                       Winter
                       Harbour   Alert Bay
TOP KNOT TACK   QUATSINO SOUND   Port McNeill   JOHNSTONE STRAIT

              Kains Island

         Brooks Peninsula
         Cape Cook
CAPE COOK SPOT

                                    Zeballos

         KYUQUOT SOUND

         NOOTKA SOUND

                    CLAYOQUOT
                    SOUND

                                                    S

                         ROLLER
                         BAY
                    NAHWITTI   Hope
NISSEN BIGHT   *BAR*   Island
NELS BIGHT   Cape   Nigei
EXPERIMENTAL BIGHT   Sutil   Island
Cape Scott   Nahwitti
GUISE BAY   River
HANSEN BAY
SEA OTTER COVE
LOWRY BAY
                                  Port
SAN JOSEF BAY   Holberg   Hardy

                    Coal Harbour   Malcolm
                                                Island
                                                  Sointula

                              Port   Alert Bay
                              McNeill
                                        Telegraph
                                        Cove

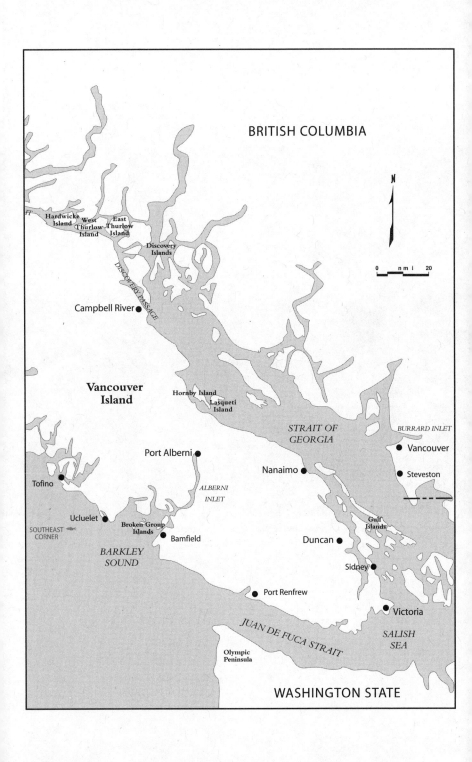

BRITISH COLUMBIA

N

0   n m i   20

Hardwicke
Island

West
Thurlow
Island

East
Thurlow
Island

Discovery
Islands

DISCOVERY PASSAGE

Campbell River ●

Vancouver
Island

Hornby Island

Lasqueti
Island

STRAIT OF
GEORGIA

BURRARD INLET

● Vancouver

Port Alberni ●

Nanaimo ●

● Steveston

Tofino ●

ALBERNI
INLET

Ucluelet ●

Broken Group
Islands

SOUTHEAST
CORNER

Bamfield ●

Gulf
Islands

Duncan ●

BARKLEY
SOUND

Sidney ●

Port Renfrew ●

Victoria

JUAN DE FUCA STRAIT

SALISH
SEA

Olympic
Peninsula

WASHINGTON STATE

We departed at dawn from the Granville Island boat basin in Vancouver's False Creek. PAUL TAYLOR

Vancouver Cast-Off

At 7:15 a.m. I untied the midships rope and leaned into the heavy wooden hull to ease her bulk from the float. Tucked the toe of my grubby sneaker into a scupper and gave the wharf a little good-riddance shove as I swung my leg over the bulwarks and onto the newly oiled deck. My feet wouldn't touch home again for four months, and that was more than fine by me. We would catch the outgoing tide that would sweep us away from this blue-collar corner of the yachty Granville Island boat basin, out into False Creek that rippled into the salty heart of the city, under the bridges and past the glittering towers and endless beaches and muscular green mountains. Out past the deep-sea freighters tethered in Burrard Inlet. Past the lighthouses and markers and buoys, then north and more north, until we reached the fishing grounds 400 miles away.

We left on a watery West Coast morning, all soft and grey and silent. Pussy-willow days, I'd called them since I'd first stood on this Vancouver wharf, clutching my dad's meaty finger in one hand and a spray of velvety grey buds in the other.

The months of preparation and fanfare behind us, Paul and I had padded back and forth piled high with the last of our baggage, the last of our fresh food and the last of our connections to this city. Anything could happen from May to October, and as it turned out, it mostly did. From the Fisheries parking lot to our old tub of a troller, along the sturdy wooden planks of the government commercial dock, up and down the steep, ribbed gangway connecting wharf to float.

By 7:20 a.m. we had our first spat, his brought on by the predictable onset of Skipper's Disease, mine by the surprising onset of apprehension. Surprising to no one but me, of course. I was going commercial salmon fishing on a wallowy old 40-foot wooden troller with a man I had known for exactly six and a half months, in some of the most dangerous waters in the world, known to modern meteorologists as The Cauldron and to centuries of boaters as the Graveyard of the Pacific.

Paul and I had been set up by a mutual friend just three days before I was leaving for a three-month trip through Europe and Egypt in the summer of 1980. Odd timing, but even odder was the fact that after my homecoming I saw him the very next day and almost every damn day after that, to the heartbreak of other hopefuls who had waited patiently for their gypsy girl to come to her senses. But Paul was a grand adventurer offering a grander adventure, and I was in love with this charming, dark-blooded man as sexy as the devil's own tail. Just into my mid-20s, I was enchanted as only a much younger woman can be, and we were gorgeous and wild as all get-out.

I decided to diffuse the earlier spat—by spat I mean he would bark at me and I would go silent then try to cheer him up—and the broody silence that followed with a quick kiss and a retreat to the deck to let that pungent sea wind blow through me.

Soothing as sympathy, erotic as a lover's breath, it had worked itself into every cell of me.

I shouldered open the thick wooden door with its port-hole window and remembered to latch the door closed. Along with everything being wet and moving, everything on an old wooden fishboat was constantly swelling and shrinking, jamming and sticking, and built to withstand a medieval battering ram. And even though this old tub was a bit of a slow pig, meaning she tended to wallow and react grudgingly to steering, she was a tough old girl.

In fairness, the *Central Isle* was already nearly 40 years old and had been built to run in inside waters as a camp tender, not a commercial salmon troller. The entire boat had been modified a few years before Paul bought her in 1979 for $90,000 including its 10-ton licence. She was no prize, but that hefty licence tonnage was the real value of the boat, and worth its weight in gold if the prices of boats and licences and fish stayed up, and the interest rates and diesel and gear prices stayed down.

I loved the old dame and was fiercely proud and protective of her, even if she did look like a pregnant whale up on the wyes in Steveston dry docks. I had spent countless hours in the last three months blowtorching and scraping and copper-painting her hull while she sat suspended. Had scrubbed the grime of the ages from every square inch of the 10-by-7-foot wooden cabin where we ate, slept, cooked, steered, laughed, tied gear, fought, pooped and made love. The cramped wheelhouse with its huge wooden steering wheel and tiny fold-down seats at each side was fronted with six narrow, heavy-framed, double-thick windows above the dashboard, racks jammed with charts, walls and ceiling with radar, depth sounder, loran and two communications radios. And right behind the seats and their half-walls, a bunk/couch on one side; cookstove, heater, sink, two narrow windows and all sizes and shapes of cupboards, drawers and bins on the other; the fold-down wood table on the back wall next to the three-inch-thick wood door with a tiny porthole. I'd corkscrewed my sturdy little self into every nook and cranny to paint everything a bright, hopeful white.

Paul insisted he re-fibreglass the hold, but I whitewashed with the heavy roller and goopy sealant 'til the injuries I tried to ignore shouted for my attention. I would prove that orthopaedic surgeon wrong: I would be as athletic and agile as before or die trying, damn it, I had told him to his face six months after the car accident that had nearly taken my life two years earlier. It was 1979, in my 24th summer. I was rear-ended in my Fiat at a red light one sunny day. I had lain in bed in a brace for months and crawled around to various therapists for a year. In the midst of the worst of it, my husband had met and bedded another woman and left to be with her. Left to escape what I'd become. A year later he begged to reconcile, when my incredible recovery revealed I was still me. I refused his offer and used part of my puny accident settlement for the tour through Europe and Egypt that helped bring me back to myself. I returned home in the fall of 1980 to a vicious divorce battle and the beginnings of a new relationship with a charming and intriguing artist-turned-fisherman. I prayed and fought and loved my way back to life out of almost unbearable loss and was going to keep my compass on true north no matter what it took.

I found a job doing in-home nursing care and took night-school courses through the winter and spring in preparation for going back to college in the coming fall of 1981 for a nursing and counselling degree. Going fishing with Paul in the spring was the perfect opportunity to earn money, have an adventure, be with him and create distance from the divorce battles at home in Vancouver. Fishing was in Paul's blood, learned at his uncle's knee in the northern BC waters near Prince Rupert. He had sold his gillnet boat for a troller just the year before. He felt gillnetting was getting too rough and competitive, and trolling seemed to be a more reasonable and humane way to make a lucrative living.

Emerging into the slowly clearing morning, I straightened my new orange Helly Hansen rain gear hanging next to Paul's beat-up ol' black ones bungeed to the cabin wall under the roof eaves. I fussed with the bin of fresh fruit and vegetables, eggs, meat and milk jammed between the four-storey, 14-inch-thick aluminum mast and the three-foot-high fibreglass hatch that opened into the cavernous hold. I strode to the end of the sloping deck and stood on the shallow wooden checker bins that would fill with fish a hundred times a day, to gaze down at the deep cockpit in the stern where I would pull in thousands of salmon and never lose one or snarl the lines and lures. The gurdy motors on either side of the cockpit that let out the steel gear lines would never jam and would always spool on and off the drums without a hitch.

Looking out at the gently rolling Strait of Georgia that would be renamed Salish Sea in honour of the First Nations peoples who had plied it for thousands of years, I asked whatever deity who would listen to keep us safe and bring us bounty. But for now, I had to ready my house.

Humming through my repertoire of Fleetwood Mac hits, I dragged the 30-pound, four-foot-square cover off the fibreglass hatch on the back deck. After gingerly lowering the bin of fresh food by rope six feet to the floor of our hold, I followed it with a ladder, then me. I could only do this because we were running through unusually calm waters. Paul would not be pleased if he knew I had clambered down here on my own while running. There are a million ways to get hurt on a boat, and every little task and action we do unthinkingly in our daily lives on land has to be recalibrated at sea, or even tied up to a wharf. No matter what it is or what you're doing, it will be wet and moving, and that includes you.

Everything on a fishboat needs to be heavy or latched down or both. I'd already seen what a heavy roll and high winds could do during a few test runs around this crazy coast and luckily, I was too naïve to know how much danger we'd really been in. In fact, the first time I'd been on the boat was when we'd first gotten together. Paul had asked me to come along with him to bring the boat home from Ucluelet harbour on the west coast of Vancouver Island. The November gales were in full force. To everyone's horror on the commercial dock, he announced we'd "just run out a bit and check it out."

Once we cleared the breakwater, the first wave heeled us over hard enough to fling open all the latched cupboards; the second knocked the pot of spaghetti off the crotchety oil stove and sent it skidding up the lino floor to the wheelhouse. By this time I was crouched on the floor like a cat, and when the third wave sent the pot skidding back, I sprang up and pinned it to the floor. Thinking the thump was some other catastrophe, Paul turned his pale, sweaty face to see me hunched over the pot, wedged against the back door. I replied to his frantic "Are you okay?" with a cheery "Don't worry, Paul, I saved the spaghetti sauce." With a whispered "Jesus!" and a shake of his head, he spun the wheel on a momentary seventh wave and ran back through the breakwater to safe harbour. People leaped to our deck from the float expecting God-knows-what. When the back door flew open and I emerged grinning and still clutching the spaghetti pot, they burst out laughing and declared that Paul had found himself a keeper.

So now, while Paul was navigating our way north, his keeper was down in the hold imagining the empty whitewashed belly of our boat filled to the brim with layer after layer of enormous gutted salmon and crushed ice. He had already constructed a small container from wooden pin boards fitted into the vertical posts running the length of the hold and thrown in crushed ice. This would serve as our refrigerator the entire time on board. No running into the kitchen to grab something from the fridge. Not only did we have to plan ahead, we had to be careful not to lose track of our groceries in the midst of a full load of ice and, hopefully, fish. I didn't have to bury the food in the ice as it was a cool spring and would get cooler the farther north we went.

Paul wasn't happy that I'd gone into the hold but softened when I told him I just wanted to do my part. Content as a broody hen, I continued clucking around the newly painted cabin I had tarted up with sunny curtains and endless scrubbing.

Lulled by the deep thrumming of the powerful Cummins diesel in the engine room under my knees and our gentle, swaying progress on the westering tide, I glanced up from stowing our precious crackers and cookies in the driest cupboard to his striking Mohican profile set in the heavy wooden frames of the four fo'c'sle windows and the endless dark treed islands and inlets. His coppery skin, ebony straight hair, jade eyes, long lithe body balanced on the balls of his feet. Watched his constant subtle checks and movements from horizon to depth sounder to loran to charts; his long artist's hands wearing the first of the season's many cuts and scabs and indelible dirt. He caught my eye as he suddenly turned from his steering perch at the wheel.

"Wow, that's a funny picture," he said, smiling crookedly.

"You look like a little kid on Christmas morning with all that stuff around you and that grin on your face and humming away. What's going on in that big head of yours?"

"I'm just thinking about how happy I am to be here and how beautiful it is out there, all misty and silvery," I said, easing back onto my heels and gazing out the little vertical window above the cookie-jar–sized sink. "I can hardly wait to see everything you've told me about and start fishing. Where are we going next?"

"Come up here to the wheelhouse and I'll show you on the chart. It's that top one on the wooden rack to the right of the dashboard. No, not that one; where the hell is it?" I chose a likely-looking candidate from the compressed stack. "Okay, that's it. Spread it out and find out where we are right now. The loran readings will give your coordinates." He pointed to the metal box flashing numbers on a black screen. "You need to learn to sight where you are on the charts by landmarks."

"I love maps," I murmured, bending close to the mass of spidery lines and numbers and convolutions and thousands of tiny islands between the 300-mile-long, pod-shaped bulk of Vancouver Island 20 miles to the west and the convoluted BC coastline reaching 1,200 miles to Alaska and the Bering Sea. "This is so cool, I can hardly wait."

"Charts, Syl, they're called charts. And tomorrow I'm going to start showing you how to tie gear if everything goes okay."

Sointula

Everything did not go okay, but I didn't care. I didn't care that Paul's self-proclaimed Taylor Curse had struck again, spewing four quarts of oil from a cracked valve onto the engine room floor, sending dashboard gauges spinning. I just got out of the way so he could yank up the floorboard in the middle of the cabin and jump down into the engine room without killing himself or me. I didn't care that the autopilot still kept pulling to starboard even after we'd paid $600 to get it fixed before we left home—I just clambered onto the skipper's seat and steered for the nearest harbour. I didn't care that we had to do an emergency run into Campbell River even though we'd already stopped in Kelsey Bay the night before to tie up and walk the four miles round trip for a beer at the only bar. I just prided myself that I could keep up with his six-foot strides. I didn't care that he spent two hours cursing and banging in the engine room. I just sat on the day bunk/couch/dining room reading Coast Salish legends and a book on Eastern religions I'd bought in Campbell River for a dollar, and handed him tools and coffee as his grimy hand poked up through the hole in the floor. I didn't care that I didn't get to learn how to tie gear yet. I just puttered and read and cooked and told stories and studied charts and stayed out of the way.

What I did care about was two days of glorious newness. I cared about watching the endless humpbacked islands slide by, the longhouses and totem poles hugging the beach in Alert Bay, the perfect moon shell found on a broken-booze-bottle beach, exploring a new place on my own. That delicious anonymous state with all senses wide open to the world. Padding through the London fog for the midnight performance of Sweeney Todd, weaving in and out of adobe galleries in Santa Fe, floating on the jade-green waters of the Seven Sacred Pools in Maui, caressing brocades in a Cairo souk.

I wanted to see and touch and hear and taste and smell everything. I wanted to know how everything worked. I was in that exquisite state of childhood curiosity that explores for the joy of it. Everything was fascinating—a bug, a boat, a brilliant sunset—and I roved to the end of whatever leash I was on—time, weather, responsibility and, occasionally, safety.

Though I had been transplanted here at the age of six from the smoke-choked industrial north of England, I was no stranger to the wilderness and working in a man's world. Dad had made sure of that. Even though my younger sibs and I grew up in Vancouver, and our father was a successful construction-business owner, I could fish by age 8, pitch a tent by 10 and build log fences and furniture by 13 at our family getaway in the BC Cariboo. My mother's voice imploring from the one-room rustic cabin, "For God's sake, Laimon, she's just a little girl." It seemed perfectly natural to whitewater canoe in the morning and go to a hip nightclub at night, to work as an engineering design draftsman and knit sweaters for my boyfriends.

It reminded me of going trolling for trout with my dad the

first time. I wore my mother's fear and worry trapped between the layers of clothing she had trowelled on me. Unable to bend my knees properly, I had slid off the log bridge on the way to the lakeshore, in the pre-dawn haze of sleepiness, and into the creek. Unable to sit upright, I had lain partially submerged like a baby seal 'til Dad sighed and shook his head, rumbling, "That woman," his ham-sized hand reaching down to pluck me from the stream.

But I wasn't six anymore, and if I went overboard I'd die. So the machine had to stretch and bend and lift and pull, faultlessly. There were no do-overs in this business. If something went wrong, the best that could happen was injury, usually serious. I couldn't afford to be a baby seal—there would be no ham-hand to pluck me from the sea. In 10 minutes I'd be dead from exposure anyway, or dragged under by my filling gumboots.

The crucible was honing me like a spear point. It's what we were designed to do before we became domestic pets. We were meant to tolerate and endure pain, exhaustion, extremes, to connect with our bodies, to use them like a tool.

Even as a toddler, I would insist, "I do it, Mummy." I had been so impatient to learn how to write and read before Grade 1 that I had enlisted my parents in a special-education program I'd devised, where they would form words by making follow-the-dots letters so I could feel like I was printing like a big girl. I hypothesized that as soon as I learned to print I would naturally be able to read and enter the magical worlds between each set of covers. I was rarely seen as pushy. Nature had taken care of that by bestowing me with a sunny disposition, multiple dimples and a loving, trusting heart . . . maybe too loving and trusting.

To really explore the world around me now, I had to view it from every possible angle. It required setting aside adult decorum and, often, personal hygiene issues. It required I be oblivious to the reactions of other adults and have a readiness to grab any opportunity that came along. It often required that I be very still and quiet and move in slow motion to sneak up on things and absorb every drop, every molecule, of the experience. The book I was reading on Eastern religions said what I had intuited long ago: Be Here Now.

After two days and 300 miles, we tied up to the pristine wharf at Sointula on Malcolm Island. The bountiful land was settled in the 1880s by Finns who were part of the wave of Scandinavian immigrants escaping poverty and desperate for land. Some homesteaded in the American Midwest, and some of the most tenacious founded utopian communities on the remote and primeval northwest coast of Canada. Finns went to Georgia Strait, Danes to Cape Scott at the northern tip of Vancouver Island, and Norwegians to Bella Coola on the mainland.

Paul and I were here to replace more damaged engine parts and fish out the sea-born plastic bags that had been sucked into the heat exchanger valve just below the water line. The innocuous shreds had damn near melted down the engine. But not even another floor removal and swear-fest could disturb a day so beautiful that things had come loose and now fluttered around inside me.

I felt spring-loaded, like my heels couldn't stand touching the ground. I knew there was something amazing very close by and I was going to find it. Paul was in the hardware store getting engine things, and the leash was off, though it didn't get much safer than Saturday afternoon in a fishing village descended from utopian Finnish settlers. The sturdy, ruddy-cheeked descendants were a picture of communal industry. Everyone was busy, brisk and friendly, and I felt like I was inside a giant wooden cuckoo clock: all moving parts and window boxes.

The wharves were like sturdy welcoming arms reaching out to sea, a stalwart mamma gathering her children home and safe, protecting them from the turbulent world. Even the private docks showed the Nordic propensity to build to last an eternity.

Drifting to the wharf edge, I marvelled at the clarity of the water (I'm sure the inhabitants would not tolerate anything less) and leaned forward to follow the lines of mighty pylons. The moment wood met water, life exploded into shape and colour. This was the treasure I was looking for. Already on my hands and knees, I leaned over as far as gravity would let me. Nature had created a marine Monet, an impressionist painting of a garden beyond imagination. If Monet could create such shimmering watery scenes from ponds and water lilies, what could he have done with this extravaganza?

Somehow, the water seemed clearer than air and acted like a magnifying glass, intensifying colour, shape and shadow. It was dazzling and hypnotic, everything in gentle motion like graceful Balinese dancers, and just as exotic. Pearly foot-long sea cucumbers, starfish like ochre suns, anemones like shaving brushes in a southwest desert. I had to remind myself that these were not gardens of alien flowers but herds of earthly animals.

They drew me down and in, as I eased myself flat on my belly, oblivious to what might be smearing my clothes or whose path I was blocking. It was not that I didn't care; I just didn't notice. The closer I got, the more I could see. And I had to see everything.

I imagined these creatures chose the high-rise housing of the pylons because it put them in the stream of whatever it was they ate. Like a buffet on a conveyor belt. And no danger of being baked before the tide rose. They clung and clustered with no thought to personal boundaries, though what territorial instincts were at play, who could tell? For all I knew it could have been all-out invertebrate warfare down there. People said that even a nuclear cloud had its own terrible beauty.

Coming from Vancouver, the marine mecca for scuba diving, I'd seen a million photos of our fabled underwater world, but nothing could have prepared me for the real thing. I now understood why divers risked their lives in our treacherous waters. But here, everything was benign beauty.

I hardly noticed I had squirmed forward in little increments. When I couldn't hold my torso like a plank anymore, I braced myself against the top of the pylons with my hand. I moved as slowly and unconsciously as my watery cousins. Personally, I thought they got all the looks in the family. The only thing I did notice after a while was that my head was throbbing and my neck was locked up again. That was about the same time I heard Paul say, "What the hell are you doing now?" and realized I was hanging upside down from my waist at the edge of a bustling commercial dock. Getting back up was not nearly as easy as slithering down, and I felt a tug on my waistband that hauled me back onto my knees. My "thank you" was swallowed up in a torrent of description, and besides, I could have gotten back up myself anyway.

As he muttered and banged the afternoon away in The Dungeon, trying to repair the damage from the oil incident and some other evil engine event, I wrote another entry in my daily journal. I had vowed to keep it faithfully. I did, as I had all my travel journals, and later added it to the velvet box that would become my personal time machine.

Now names of the jumbled islands from the Inside and Discovery Passages tumbled onto the page from the folded chart as I marked our progress north, fraught with breakdowns. Lasqueti, Hornby, Quadra, Sonora, East and West Thurlow, Hardwicke, Malcolm. Discovery Passage bore the name of Captain Vancouver's sailing ship that had brought Europeans to the Salish world between Vancouver Island and the fjordy mainland.

I tried to keep writing through the rolly slop out of Sointula, and though my stomach stayed right where it was meant to, the pen wouldn't, and I had to stow my journal in its prescribed spot in the chart rack under the loran. It was only an hour's run directly across the narrow strait to scraggy little Port McNeill, but we were thrown around a bit and many a hapless sailor would have lost his lunch. Even Paul was queasy the first few days of every season. Some people never got over it, puking themselves inside out before running or being dragged off a fishboat. The local seasick saying was that for the first week you're scared you're gonna die, and for the second, you're scared you won't. I had inherited a freakishly stable inner ear from my sturdy Nordic father, who had braved the north Atlantic one January in the mid '50s on a rickety tramp steamer to Halifax from Bristol. My aristocratic Florentine mother, on the other hand, would barf at the sight of the sea or in any moving object, as would my poor younger sister.

The only sea-related issues I had was what I called the Land Wavies, which didn't make me barf, just kept me wavering as if I was still on board but settled down as soon as I'd slept. My non-barfiness also contributed to my being a keeper and a prized female deckhand. Prized because we were famed to be cleaner, smarter, tougher, soberer, pleasanter than our male counterparts and we worked like bloody demons. The question, though, was always this: would she or wouldn't she? Is she or isn't she? Ten percent if she didn't, and 15 percent if she did.

Paul had the ideal situation: a potentially top-notch deckhand who *would* and *did* without that unfortunate issue of keeping her existence, or the reason for the extra five percent, from The Wife . . . For all intents and purposes I was a wife, and therefore only got 10 percent. Not much if you're trying to conjure up enough money to go back to university, especially when 10 percent of nothing is nothing.

I may have been a willing and hearty bedmate, but my fantasies of highjinks on the high seas were already fading like fog as Paul insisted on sleeping on the day bunk "to keep an eye on things." Meanwhile, I was firmly directed to one of the two narrow bunks on the port side of the curving, wedge-shaped space of the bow, three steps down from our main living area, right below the wheelhouse and behind the bulwarks that separated it from the engine room. To complete this palatial bedroom was a cupboard along the opposite bow wall, a narrow two-foot bench with a lid that doubled as a locker, and a teeny-tiny toilet that you pumped to swish away the unmentionables straight out to the chuck. All this in the space of an apartment-size walk-in closet.

We were four days out and now tied up at the government Fisheries dock in Port McNeill for another long night of frantic engine repairs. As I reached again for my journal, I stood transfixed by the sultry moon and sea of stars framed in the fo'c'sle window. I was struck by how much I wanted Paul's body next to me at night. Felt the first worry over the latest reports of bad weather and poor fishing; the first pangs of a loneliness that would grow tall inside me then work itself in deep.

After a flurry of journaling and a bracing cup of tea, I flopped belly down on the floor and hung my head over the hole to hand him a wrench as he continued his hand-to-hand combat with the Cummins.

"Hey, I forgot to tell you, I had the strangest thing happen yesterday when I was steering while you were ripping the pilot to bits on the hatch cover."

"Uh, yeah? What?"

"It was so weird. I was just sitting there, keeping the compass marker right where you told me and watching for logs and junk in the water. And I was just staring out at the grey horizon and the grey sky and the grey water and it was so calm in the channel."

"Hmm-hmmmm . . . Oh shit! Ah, sorry, go on."

"I wasn't really thinking of anything and I felt so peaceful and calm, and all of a sudden this song I wrote when I was a kid in high school just started floating through my head—I could hear my voice and my guitar. I heard it clear as day and I haven't even thought of it for probably 10 years. I couldn't have remembered the words to save my life and suddenly there it was, like a little concert in my head."

"Yuh, I've had things like that happen before. All kinds of strange stuff happens in your head when you're out on the water. What's the song about? Can you hand me the Phillips screwdriver? No, the other one; I mean the *longer* one. God, this piece-of-shit boat is driving me nuts. We're going to have to go into Port Hardy tomorrow to get a new heat exchanger valve and get the pilot checked. One more day down the tubes to the Taylor Curse."

I offered another grubby screwdriver that looked like it could lever up a tank. "Yeah, that's the one, thanks. You were saying?"

"Just a sec, my neck is bugging me. I gotta lay on my side. Okay. It was about the ocean being the Mother of everything. 'Member I told you about those guys I met a few years ago through my social worker friends who worked at that Indian residence between Ucluelet and Tofino? Who were going to use my songs for a documentary about environmental issues on the BC coast?"

"Uhhhh, yuh. Hang on, I have to bang this rusty nut to get it loose. Okay, go ahead. So, what about the song? "

"Well, okay, I could sing it for you."

Pretty Lady, lovely Lady
Oh Mother
Mother of us all

One sad day, I went to the shoreline
So lonely and afraid, I could have cried
Then She called to me, with a voice like a choir
A thousand seagulls, soaring higher

And though your waves may toss
And though your fury kills
You're Mankind's Mother
And always will

One by one you'll claim us
Back to your womb, from when we came
Lying in our eternal sleep
With you once again

And though your waves may toss . . .

And I did, every word. On my belly with my head hanging down into the engine room, as the skies darkened, and the seagulls stilled, with the faint sounds of Elton John and drunken conversations floating down from the bar up the hill. While Paul sat back on his heels, grimy hands at rest. His upturned face lit from more than the bare bulb hanging from its cord on the engine room wall.

Port Hardy

The Cauldron of the northern BC coast is just what the meteorologists' name implies: a bubbling, primeval soup of massive tides; deadly reefs, shelves and pinnacles; towering mountains; sudden shallows; torturous narrows; and open seas all the way north to Alaska and west to Japan. Frigid Bering Sea currents and air hurl themselves into the balmy south Pacific waters and trade winds sweeping up from Japan and Mexico. A combination of any of these at any time can explode into a roiling boil and create storms of epic proportions. Winds of 200 miles per hour have been clocked at Cape Scott at the northern tip of Vancouver Island—seas that would swallow a four-storey building.

Scientists from all over the world come to study this phenomenon of nature's unfathomable power. It's a restless, unpredictable, untameable world that terrifies some and enchants others. It reminds us daily who is really in charge. It seduces us with gentle beauty then explodes into terrifying rages. Some people can't bear feeling so insignificant and others find it a blessed relief. This is no place for control freaks and egotists, but it is just the right place for the wild hearts, the romantics and the eccentrics. There is space and tolerance and sometimes affection for even the squarest pegs.

For most of us, it wasn't just a way to make money or run from conformity; it was the call of the wild, the last great frontier of our great country that still rang with the ancient songs lodged deep in our bones. We were here to be a part of something so much greater than the domesticated life of the urban treadmill and to continue the tradition of our courageous ancestors and people throughout history who had chosen the unknown, the devil they didn't know, over the safety of the mundane. Something that would last who knows how long, but probably not as long as we hoped.

The Cauldron had gone from a simmer to a bubble overnight with a marine forecast for a bit of a boil by that night. The clanging of riggings and uneasy shifting of boats before first light dragged us from our separate beds to make the 22-mile run from Port McNeill to Port Hardy before things got nasty. I was not by nature an early riser, but I loved the simple choreography of morning we had already fallen into: Paul would start the engine and turn up the oil stove in the galley to boil water; I would dress quickly and come upstairs to make coffee; he would start up all the radios and electronics; I would make sure everything was secured inside and out using a checklist I had devised; he would untie the bow and stern line and pull up the bumpers hanging on ropes that protected the hull from the float; I would untie the midships line and wait for his signal from the wheelhouse to push the boat out a bit then jump on deck with the rope.

I was a vertical-learning-curve kind of girl and had always detested standing on the sidelines of anything, so I asked Paul for more and more to do so I could feel useful and a part of things. He would mete out tasks and information bit by bit: what an underwater pinnacle looked like on the depth sounder, steering left to go right and right to go left, how to light the cantankerous oil stove, that a little port left in the bottle meant that starboard was on the right, how to read the tide book for highs and lows, and the brief slacks in between when you could safely run the narrows and shallows. I chafed under the slowness of my learning and always snuck in a little extra something. It was hard for him to stay mad at me when something was beyond me, like tying gear, because I was so damn smart and earnest about it and it did take more of the workload off him. At times, though, I slid right past competent worker to over-eager puppy and, occasionally, into just plain stupid risk-taker. Like when he had told me in no uncertain terms to never pull up the trolling poles alone because they were too heavy and came out of the cabin to find me dangling six feet above the deck, still hanging onto the rope and slowly swinging back and forth.

We slipped out of Port McNeill's choppy bay and around the corner of Malcolm Island, coffee and cigs firmly in hand, and into a mounting lump that signalled our first foray out of the sheltered Inside Passage into the relatively open waters of Broughton Strait. By Port Hardy, we would be in Queen Charlotte Strait and full on to the winds and water finally let loose and funnelling down the coast from Alaska, diverted and maddened by the Queen Charlotte Islands, which would wait another 30 years to be renamed Haida Gwaii.

It kicked up fast and mean, so we ran full throttle with stabilizers up to squeeze out the *Central Isle*'s maxed-out running speed of eight knots. The stabilizers were used primarily while fishing at a two-knot speed to ease the boat's movement, but they were also used to run in heavy, dangerous seas, although they slowed the boat considerably. Fishermen often gambled the risks and benefits in a high-stakes decision to sacrifice speed or stability.

But these were hardly ideal conditions and eight knots is pretty slow even for a troller. Knots and nautical miles are hangers-on from the days of the old sailing ships, when a sea mile was based on one minute of latitude. The length of one minute of latitude is 1.85 kilometres, or 1.15 miles. A vessel travelling at one knot along a line travels one minute of latitude in one hour. The nautical mile is about one minute of latitude along any line. Originally, sailing ship speed was calculated by how many knots on a rope attached to a board flung overboard would pass a mark on the stern in 30 seconds measured by a sand-filled hourglass.

This was the kind of information I devoured while running, along with the stash of books under my bunk and anything else that caught my interest. It was the best way to sublimate our pitching and rolling, Paul's almost-daily temper tantrums in the engine room and his brooding over the early reports of lousy fishing. Besides, I really couldn't do anything else when it was rough. I'd either wreck something or myself or both. The most productive thing I could do was read or journal or daydream, or endlessly study the charts. The view didn't exactly inspire: everything a dark, mean-looking grey. The lump turned into sharp, crested waves. Spray came over the bow and splattered the wheelhouse windows. Even the coastline seemed to cower like a scared dog.

Before I dove into my book, I thought I'd check in with The Skipper, and slid off the day bunk to crab-walk the six feet to where he stood steering and staring intently through the spray-mottled windows in the wheelhouse—a silly name, as it was just the front end of the same space as the galley. I gripped the dashboard shelf edge and planted my feet far apart to stay put and spoke matter-of-factly, as if we were lounging in our apartment kitchen back home instead of bouncing around on the northern ocean.

"Would you like something to eat or more coffee or something?"

"Uh, it's a bit rough through here until we get to Hardy in a couple of hours."

"How about a sandwich? You can't go without anything."

"No thanks."

"Crackers and cheese? I put some in the kitchen sink before we left and I won't cut anything, just break off a chunk."

"Okay fine. Can you get another pack of cigarettes from the cupboard too? God, I've got to cut down. What are you reading?" He stole a quick glance at the day bunk to the striking black and green cover. "*Daughters* of what?"

"*Copper Woman*. It's written by a woman named Ann Cameron who lives on the Sunshine Coast and interviewed all these Native elders about their myths and legends and wrote this incredible book. I've just read a couple, but they're amazing. Reminds me of when I was volunteer-teaching West Coast Ethnology once a week at the Vancouver Museum to school kids with Connie. You know her—my Cree friend in North Van. When I was recovering from the car accident, after I could walk around. God, I'll never forget the look on their faces when I showed up in my big neck brace for the orientation."

"Pretty brave. Did they ever charge the guy who hit you?"

"Just a sec. I'm gonna get the crackers and cheese and bring them up here," I said, and crabbed over to the sink, grabbed the goods and some paper towel and crabbed back.

"Here, I'll put yours right in front of you. And no, they never did charge him. His top-notch lawyer got him off. Since he was driving a company car he didn't even have to pay higher premiums. Anyway, the next story in the book is about a terrible sea monster called Sisiutl, and facing your fears."

"Well, let's hope we don't meet him today," he said, taking a bite of cheese and turning up the marine radio for the continuous weather forecast.

We pulled into the relief of Hardy Bay about the time most people in the other world were sipping morning coffee in their pyjamas. I had been up for hours and had already rodeo-rode a rising gale and got my first dose of the frontier town of Port Hardy. Everything and everybody seemed as restless and rough as the weather, stirred up by the swirling masses of men and the occasional woman who carved a life from the seas and woods and rocks. Fishermen, loggers and miners kept to their own kind, and even within those tribes, there were smaller packs. No self-respecting troller Swivelhead would hang out with a gillnet Ragpicker or a Circlejerk Insaner purse-seiner. And nobody went near the draggers, whose massive apparatus scraped the ocean bottom raw, or the dog fishermen, who smelled like hell's privy. Part of this was the human tendency to run with our own kind, but the truth was, we were all competing for the same fish. 'Specially this year when catch numbers were coming in low and there were rumours of hikes in fuel and interest rates and rumblings about sport-fishing camps and fish farms appearing in sheltered inlets and bays all over the coast.

Trollers considered themselves the elite of the salmon fishermen. They were restricted to fishing at least a mile offshore, and there was a certain gentility about quietly dragging hooks through the water away from stream and river mouths. Their surgically dressed and gently handled fresh fish were the elite of the marketplace, destined for artfully arranged displays in fish shops and chi-chi foodie boutiques.

The *sportys* and *yachtys* were restricted to the public dock and so were naturally kept separate from the lowlife fishermen. (We wouldn't be called the gender-friendly but clumsy *fisherperson* and then the sensible *fisher* for some years yet.) If a pleasure boat did try to sneak into a commercial float, they could be reported to the wharfinger or harbourmaster. He would ask them to move, and if they refused he was authorized to call the RCMP. As competition for tie-up space heightened over the years, altercations would blow up with threats of legal action from both sides, especially if there happened to be an American accent or boat involved.

We wandered the Port Hardy commercial docks and waited for the electronics repair shop to open, hoping to get our pilot fixed that day while we were kept in port by the weather. Four days had slid by already, and without a pilot I would have to sit in the cabin all day steering the long, slow tacks back and forth on the fishing grounds while Paul worked the gear on deck. I would do what needed to be done but was restless to get out there in the stern and really fish. I wanted to do the real stuff: play with the boys, run with the Big Dogs, or the *highliners* in this case. There was nothing more demeaning than being referred to as a *lowliner*, someone who barely scratched out a living and had to struggle to make the dreaded mortgage payment and licence renewal fees every year. And the federal government's good ol' Unemployment Insurance Commission (UIC) purse strings were beginning to tighten, offering little solace to a seasonal worker who relied on financial support through the winter.

The glory days when a fisherman could take it easy over the winter and enjoy some down time would soon be over. A lot of outsiders were beginning to see this as *ripping off the system* and often lumped all fishermen into the same group that appeared to work the occasional 24- to 48-hour opening, goofed off the rest of the time and made a killing. A distorted view of net fishermen and completely untrue of trollers, who worked up to 18 hours a day for 10 to 12 days straight with one or two days' turnaround at the fish camps in incredibly dangerous and exhausting conditions for four or five months. Even though the trolling season ran from mid-April to the end of October in 1981, the first and last month or two were often just too unpredictable and rough with bad weather. But no one could have imagined the industry would be in such conflict and peril that by the mid-'90s the seasons would be down to eight weeks and sometimes six.

So as the season lengths and catchments steadily decreased over the years, and UIC was becoming damn near impossible to get, it got harder and harder to survive—and many did not. What the restrictions did do was gradually hone a fleet of savvy, entrepreneurial career fishermen. In 1981 there were 1,600 BC trollers working the entire coast from north of the Queen Charlottes to the southern Gulf Islands; 20 years later there would be 540.

And it seemed the entire fleet was here in Port Hardy now, jamming the wharves and floats, waiting out the weather and as restless as we were to get their season going.

I was awestruck by the bald eagles that scrounged around

every foot of shoreline and mud flat and their massive nests in every tree with a decent horizontal branch.

"Thick as seagulls," Paul said. "You'll get used to it. It's a shock to see them, coming from the city. This is how it used to be everywhere, but you have to get this far north now to see them like this."

I didn't ever want to get used to it, or the feral forests and waters that crouched just behind every human settlement carved out of this remaining wilderness.

We waited out the weather and the hours of diagnosis on the pilot by having our first official gear-tying lesson in the cabin. The drop-down Arborite table attached to the back wall turned the day bunk from dining room to workshop as boxes of shoe-sized silver flashers and coppery little spoons and a rainbow of rubbery squid-like hoochies piled up, along with hooks, tiny clamp-stops, bright beads, swivels and spools of 50-pound test transparent Perlon fishing line. It was all I could do not to start making jewellery out of this gorgeous stuff.

We were only tying gear to attract spring salmon and what-ever sockeye showed up, because those were the only two of the five salmon species open to trollers this early. The Department of Fisheries and Oceans (DFO) set the species openings, and in later years the catch-numbers, in keeping with whatever calibrated voodoo equations they came up with to regulate an industry that was already careening into decline. But this year, coho season didn't open until July 1, and pinks not until August 1, so if we did hook one before then we had to shake it off (hence the barbless hooks). The *drowned* ones were whisked into our oil-stove oven. Chum salmon were fall runners and mostly caught by net fishermen. A troller could still fish anywhere on the coast, inside or outside waters, for any species (according to openings), then slap on a drum and go gillnetting in the fall. By 1995 the DFO and its Round Table restrictions narrowed the window of opportunity to a porthole. Trollers, who were hardest hit from every direction, were left stunned and angry and asking questions: Why was the most viable, sustainable fishery type being systematically beaten down? Why were fish farms and sport-fishing camps taking over every good anchorage on the coast? Battle lines were being drawn and every user group was ready to fight it out. But some had louder voices than others, and those voices were heard by more powerful ears.

A tense restlessness filled the cabin and I learned to tie gear as fast as I possibly could to keep the polite and distant communication from blowing up. I would be the best gear-tier ever: an arm's length of line attached with a three-wrap knot pulled tight with spit to the swivel so the flasher would spin in the water; then half an arm of line, another swivel, a spoon, a bead, then a green hooch with the line passed through end to end and tied to a barbless hook; then the hooch pushed down to almost cover the hook with its fluttering tentacles.

"You're doing okay but some of your knots aren't tight enough," Paul said, "so I'll have to redo them or the gear will just unravel in the water. No, I'll do it. Your hands aren't strong enough or toughened up enough yet and the line is starting to cut your hands. Bad news when you're working with fish."

Did I feel bad about luring a fish to its death? No, but I *did* feel bad that I couldn't tie the knots tight enough—yet. I had been fishing with my dad since I was eight—ironically, mostly lake trolling—and I could bait a hook with a live worm, reel in the trout, conk him over the head and gut him out for the fry pan. Dad used to joke that he stopped taking me fishing cuz it was too embarrassing getting skunked by a little girl. We had the Kodaks to prove it, especially the one where he grinned sheepishly into the camera with his one little rainbow trout while I stood proud as hell with a string of speckled beauties. I didn't know it, but those long, quiet days with Dad puttering up and down a lake not only were precious then but were filling a deep well I would draw from for the rest of my life.

Suddenly a familiar voice called from the float. "Hey, Paul, Syl, you at home?" Boat etiquette insists on a call-out before stepping on the deck, a knock on the door, even if it's open, and no entry until invited.

"Richard! Steve!" I bounded out the door and onto the float to give our friend and his strapping good-natured deckhand from Vancouver a huge hug and cheek-kiss.

"Hey sweetie, good to see you, you little pipsqueak," Steve said in his mellowed New Yorkese and held me at arm's length. "You look happy and healthy as always, so things must be going well. Where's the old man?"

"Hey, good to see you too," Paul said smiling in the doorway, broodiness all forgotten. "We're just about to go check on the pilot. Wanna get together for dinner tonight?"

"I'll make spaghetti," I chimed in. It was the only thing we could afford. With their bread and salad we would feast and laugh and tell stories and ignore the howling gale and that "asshole electronics guy" who hadn't fixed the pilot and couldn't get to it for days because he was so busy and needed a part he didn't have, and the pilot should be replaced anyway cuz it was getting too old. And we'd ignore that the little bit of money we scrounged to get here was almost used up by fuel and repairs and we still had to get to the BC Packers fish camp in Bull Harbour on Hope Island a few more hours north. We would leave exploring Hardy's handful of streets and infamous hotel bars, the wharf-side Seagate and the *uptown* Thunderbird, for another trip. I had a feeling they would out-weird and out-rough even the crazy bars in the outposts of Ucluelet and Tofino on Vancouver Island's west coast. We needed to start fishing and making some money very, very soon, and if the weather calmed down the next day, we would head up to Bull Harbour and do just that. That night in my bunk I felt like an arrow vibrating with energy and ready to spring from the bow.

Bull Harbour

I thought Italians were intense! My mother had nothing on Mother Nature, who had cleaned house overnight in a fury of wind and rain until even this tawdry little town shone and fluttered in the soft morning light. All the sullen grey had been swept and scoured away to reveal a world transformed. She had trotted out her best greens and blues and sparkling whites to show off her lovely home as if in preparation for company.

We sped over the rippling bay and out into the stunningly calm Goletas Channel that would lead us another three hours north to Bull Harbour. I mused on what Mother Nature might be celebrating today and leaned against Paul in companionable silence as he sat and steered the boat. My eyes drifted from the hypnotic sparkling seas over to the Royal Bank calendar, a few feet to my right, thumbtacked to the varnished wall of the wheelhouse under the depth sounder. May's picture was a Saskatchewan wheat farmer seeding his endlessly rolling furrowed land, and here I was in another world, yet the same country. Amazing. Not so different, really: he was making his living from the land too. We were both working to feed the world. Working from the sweat of our brows with nature's rhythms and bounties in a simple, honest way—it doesn't get much nobler than that. I was just about to remark on this when I suddenly snapped to attention.

"Holy shit, Paul, it's Mother's Day! I can't believe we've only been gone five days. It feels like five months. Look, it's May 18th. I've got to get hold of Mum and Dad to let them know I'm okay. She will be freaking. Is there a phone at the camp I could use and reverse charges?"

"We'll have to see when we get there. The camp is barged in every year by tugs and things can change. Depends on who's managing and if they have a decent connection after that storm. Maybe you can ask the manager if you can use his phone real quick. He might be sympathetic to a cute girl who wants to call her mum on Mother's Day," he said with a grin.

We did have some capacity for long-distance calls on our radio telephone, but it was incredibly expensive, especially to Clinton, in the Cariboo region of BC's interior where my parents had retired. It was only for extreme emergencies because the call would have to go through the Coast Guard and be patched into BC Tel. I had told my mum that if they ever received a patched call it would be very serious, which had reduced her to heartbreaking tears. There were other phones that could be patched straight into the telephone system, but they were a fortune and, needless to say, we couldn't afford one—or the calls.

My mother, who had suffered through countless sleepless nights over my adventures, had been completely beside herself when I told her and Dad that I was going commercial fishing with Paul up north. Whitewater canoeing for a weekend was one thing, but a boat in the middle of nowhere, where every imaginable (and she had a great imagination) thing could maim or kill you in an instant? That was more than she could bear. She had already seen and experienced unimaginable suffering and destruction growing up in northern Italy during the Second World War and knew all too well what could happen to a human being. And I was her baby, the first-born, her only link to my father when they were separated for long periods and distances in their early years together. She had already endured the loneliness and isolation as a beautiful young woman coming to Canada and living alone with a child in Edmonton, then fledgling Vancouver, while my father toiled in constant danger in remote lumber camps in northern Alberta, then northern Vancouver Island, before forming a successful construction company.

As a tow-headed farm boy, my father had been flung into the horrors of fighting for his beloved Latvia and then into camps as a Displaced Person. He later followed his heart as a gifted musician and arranger in northern England, where he met and married my mother and I was born. And now they were two middle-aged mismatched folks living quietly in the middle of 160 acres of high pine forest in the middle of the Big Bar ranching district where my father had finally found home.

He was not frightened or worried about me, believing in his deep Nordic heart that Mother Nature would always keep me safe and bring me home to him again. He hung on every word of my colourful stories, sky-blue eyes shining with chip-off-the-old-block pride. Before the fishing season, the last thing he'd said when he crushed me in his hug was "Remember to call your mother—this is going to be tough for her. Write me a letter now and again. You write as good as you talk."

If I'd known how early he would be taken from us, I'm not sure I would have let that hug go. But what he held closest to his heart was knowing that I carried his spirit of survival and a hunger for life.

"Hey, how about rustling up some grub, there, deckie," Paul said, smiling, and jerked his thumb over his shoulder to the galley. "That porridge ain't gonna cook itself and we have another couple of hours before we get to Bull Harbour."

"Aye-aye, Captain Honey." I saluted smartly.

"I'll have ye keelhauled for insubordination."

"You'll have to catch me first," I said, relieved that his brooding had lifted. He and Mother Nature had a lot in common.

Keeping the cranky old oil stove on an even keel was an art and a science in itself, similar to turning lead into gold. It was either blasting hot or barely warm and went out completely when it got rough. My experience drawing machine-engineering spec sheets for a living was definitely coming in handy now, if for nothing else than to save me from being completely mystified.

While he ate at the wheel, I took my bowl out to the deck and sat on the hatch cover in my jeans, gumboots and three sweaters, and watched my Brave New World open up and slide by. Land gave way to sea and horizon, at times completely—a very odd thing for a girl brought up in a city of mountains and rivers and the high sierras of the BC Interior. I was no stranger to the waters by canoe and sailboat, but the next five months were as unknowable as the ocean horizon that revealed the curvature of the earth.

Entering Bull Harbour off Goletas Channel was like one of those old King Kong movies where people stumbled upon a secret world tucked away from time and the familiar. Just when

I thought we'd be flung out into the wild open seas beyond the channel, we slipped into a subtle little opening that wound a bit left, then right, and suddenly stunned us with a spacious bay carved into the port side of Hope Island—the last stop on the way to the Queen Charlotte Islands, two treacherous days north.

Glassy water reflected the low-slung land furred with trees dwarfed by powerful winds. Today it was a bustling place of fishboats loading and unloading, coming and going, from the two enormous barges that held an entire fish camp of ice houses, storage, general store, office, fuel tanks, water systems and floats. The portable factory town was owned and operated by BC Packers, the biggest and oldest commercial fish handler since the late 1800s.

I was like a terrier, scurrying around the deck to see everything all at once. Since the space along the floats was limited, we could tie up at the servicing dock only to unload fish or take on ice, fuel and water. Lots of boats had to anchor out in the bay, away from the clamour and the company. While the more reclusive folks preferred this, most fishermen tended to be friendly and sought out human contact and conversation like a Bedouin would an oasis.

Bull Harbour was the only fish camp north of Hardy, the entire top end, and for a hundred miles down the west side of Vancouver Island. The only place for fuel or water or the precious crushed ice that kept your dressed fish from turning to rotten mush over 10 or 12 days before offloading and uploading for the next stint—a blur of action called The Turnaround. Every day lost to weather or breakdown or hangover was a financial loss, never mind the exhaustion or injury.

After we registered our logbook, names and social insurance numbers at the office and made nice with the new managers, we spent the last of our money on diesel, cigs and a coveted chocolate bar, then filled up the sectioned bins with crushed ice and topped up the teeny water tank. After lunch Paul started the Talk Circuit. He strolled the floats, checked in with old friends, caught up on rumours and gossip, greeted strangers and occasionally remembered to introduce me. In time I would get accustomed to and even learn to ignore the bold stares, usually from older fishermen, the leering inquiries about whether I was looking for a job and the predictable curiosity about Paul and my personal status. But it was still early in the season and the men not long from their homes, so all was tolerable. Many of Paul's pals were genuinely warm and friendly, welcoming me to the industry and acting almost courtly. Some of them would become very dear to me, and welcome havens in the tough days to come.

I hadn't had so much coffee and nicotine since college, and between the chemical buzz and the excitement of starting fishing the next day, I was getting pretty jingly. Paul suggested we row to the back of the bay and hike across the narrow neck of woods to Roller Bay. Dave, the camp manager, hadn't been too keen to let me use their phone to call my parents, but Marji, his sweetheart of a wife, melted like Mother's Day chocolate and said I could make a quick call after dinner that night when things had slowed down at the camp. With a quick hug to her, we were off in our skiff to explore.

We made for the crossed trees that marked the trailhead. Bathed in warm sun and Paul's assurances we'd only be gone a couple of hours, we brought nothing to eat or drink and wore only sweatshirts, jeans and sneakers. Full of fun and frolics, we set off at a jaunty pace until we came to a fork in the trail just inside the dense pine forest that rose like a fortress behind the scrub and salal of the waterfront. It was a toss-up which way to go. Since Paul couldn't remember which side to take and both paths were equally untrodden and vague, that's what we did: tossed a coin. Seemed like pretty much everything else was up to the whims of fate, so why not this too? We took the right fork and hoped for the best. How far could it be? We could already hear a faint rumbling, which we took to be the surf.

Padding along the spongy trail we fell into a silent, dreamy rhythm, lulled by the pulse of life around us. Vegetation didn't just grow in the rainforest, it vibrated and hummed in a million shades of green so intense we could almost taste the chlorophyll. And today was particularly symphonic since it wasn't being lashed by wind and rain for a change.

If the forest was Gaia the Earth Goddess's heart, then the ocean was her breath, the draw of her mighty bellows. Growing louder 'til it resonated in every cell like a tuning fork. Some pre-paleolithic part of us heard and knew we were going home and prepared to slide back to meet it.

We stepped through the dark velvet curtain and onto a dazzling stage where another kind of Passion play unfolded: the marriage of sea and sky. It swallowed our jokes and glibness and all our silly little human concerns. We were blown out fresh and flat and simple as white sheets in the wind.

The waves rumbled us quiet, as we lay side by side on this beach at the edge of nowhere. The waves whispered us to sleep after we made love and nestled deep into our warm, pebbly mattress like salmon and dreamed our fishy dreams.

We awoke suddenly to the bellowing waves as we stirred and blinked in our chilly hard beds. The sun was racing for the horizon, kicking up spumes of smoky dust and setting the clouds smouldering. If we didn't hurry, it would get home before we did. A moonlit trail may be romantic in Vancouver's Stanley Park, but it was deadly out here.

Scrambling up the gravelly slope, we ran back and forth looking for the trailhead, like terriers looking for a rabbit hole. After a few false starts we found something familiar enough to call a trail and convinced ourselves it was the right one. It was not. We knew it but wouldn't admit it. Where it had been spongy, it was now boggy. Where it had been lush, it was now forbidding with dark looming trees, massive ferns and dense tangled underbrush. The cool dappled light now blurred and ran together.

The more we needed to hurry, the slower we had to go—like trying to run in a dream. Like running underwater. I thought of those experiments I'd read about where people could actually breathe oxygen-suffused water without drowning. Maybe this was one of nature's experiments, an attempt at creating another element. Everything seemed so saturated that one more drop and this whole place would burst into water. Soon we couldn't step over or around the dark water. The pools ate up every inch of ground and the humus became porridge.

Even if we had been able to pick our way around the water and bog, it was blanketed by an endless morass of fallen trees, helter-skelter like a giant game of pick-up sticks. Most of them had been here long enough to grow thick shaggy coats of slippery moss, playing host to the next generation of flora. I looked down at my flimsy tennis shoes and prayed they would magically grow golfing spikes. There was no way around, just through.

We tried to keep moving in some general direction while zigzagging from one slightly more stable surface to another with the concentration of tightrope walkers. Though the moss underfoot was an enemy, the stuff hanging on live trees was a friend, showing us where north was in this surrealistic world. Or so we hoped.

Lost in some *Alice In Wonderland* fantasy, it seemed that the trees and ferns and moss had not gotten bigger but we had become smaller—I was certain of it. We had become four-footed, big-eyed, furry little mammals scurrying from one fallen tree to the next, criss-crossing this forbidding primeval swamp to find their burrow trail. Ears pricked for the sound of crashing reptiles, we wordlessly pushed on, saving our energy and breath, with only an occasional grunt to indicate a safer or shakier footing.

I wondered if we were really just wandering aimlessly and for how long our exhausted legs could hold out. How ironic, I thought, after everything we've been through, to die in a rain-forest swamp less than two miles from our skiff and the lights of the fish camp. If we didn't succumb to exposure—May up here was like March in Vancouver—we could slip off any one of these fallen logs and break a leg or rip our guts open on a spike or be swallowed up by bog mud.

But that was just bogeyman talk. I didn't know about Mr. Ace Explorer, but I was going to make it back okay; I always would. I could feel Paul glancing at me to gauge my fear or resentment. He found none. I felt no fear because I had yet to experience its profound power. This was another challenge to be met and conquered, and I would be my father's daughter. I took an almost perverse pleasure in survival. The car accident and my agonizing recovery had become my new benchmark.

Paul didn't apologize or make excuses or try to help or reassure me. I had wanted equality in a man's world and I was getting it, though I wanted some small token of love or pride or gratitude: a tender embrace, a *you did great*, an *I'm a lucky man* or a *thanks for being such a damned good sport*.

According to my father, I was one of nature's beloveds, and as such, the Nature Spirits would always protect me. And they did, then and countless times to come.

"What are you smiling about?" Paul said in the dimming light.

"Everything," I said as a faint trail appeared in the soggy ground.

"Daddy, can you hear me? You have to remember to say *over*," I shouted into the mouthpiece at the fish camp office and forgot to say the critical *over* so he would know when to speak.

"There is no problem with the line," he rumbled in his lilting accent. "But your mother is crying so hard I can hardly hear you. Angela, for God's sake, calm down. Everything good here, except for your mother worrying herself sick about you. Lots of action around here lately. Your sister had her baby five days ago, another little girl. Your mother is pushing for Lisa Gay. It's good you called for Mother's Day, Sylvi."

I heard my mother's sobs and her burbled "Let me talk, Laimon." My calm resolve started to melt away. My eyes filled with tears at my father's voice and my mother's sobs and I swallowed over and over to keep my voice steady. My little sister was a mummy again and my throat ached with nostalgia. I was an auntie again and I had missed my niece coming into the world. I remembered the boundless joy of holding Jenny, Gay's firstborn, in my arms just two years before, still bloody and slippery from the womb. Tears escaped. That world and that life already seemed surreal, like that was the movie and this was real life.

"Sweetheart, it's Mum. I've been so worried about you; are you alright?" she sobbed. "Just before you called I was sitting in the living room and thinking of you and when I was pregnant with you in England. I just found out and was so happy and Daddy was so worried because he wanted to wait until we went to Canada to have a baby. But I wanted you so badly, *mia cara,* and there I was on Mother's Day, knitting you a little pink sweater, *piccola bella bambina,* because I just knew you would be a beautiful little girl. Born in January, my birthday present. And there you are now, grown up and so far away and doing something so dangerous. Are you okay? Tell me the truth. When am I supposed to say *over*?" Mum dissolved again in sobs, and with that came my own tears.

I didn't know radio telephones broadcasted to every single person dialled into that frequency, which in this case was every person in the fleet, plus anyone anywhere near the external speakers at the fish house. The manager and his wife had discreetly moved to the next room. It wasn't until Paul came into the office and signalled that it was time to end the call and we were walking down the long outside wooden stairway to the dock that he told me the reason people were snickering all along the way to our boat. I wasn't even remotely mortified, having grown up with an emotive mum, but laughed so hard I teared-up and could hardly climb onto the boat. Paul, a tad embarrassed, said people would be chuckling about the incident for days. I said I thought it was often safer to laugh over something than to cry, especially in this world where we had to keep a tight rein on our emotions.

I would come to understand how that became a survival mechanism for most people living dangerous lives.

We went to bed early, thinking that would give us the good night's sleep we would need for our first day of fishing. But sleep would elude us as we lay in our separate bunks, mine from excitement, his from worry.

First Day Fishing

My psychic requisition for our first day of fishing must have gotten mixed up with someone else's, because instead of a beautiful calm day filled with spring salmon flying over the stern and into the checkers, we got someone's request for a day in hell. There is an old Yiddish proverb that says: *If you want to make God laugh, make a plan.* God was having a real knee-slapper.

We tiptoed out of Bull Harbour at 5:30 a.m. with a few other brave souls who decided to tough out the reports of rising wind and seas coming down from the north. Hitting Goletas Channel after the sheltered calm of the bay was like being grabbed off the sidewalk and thrown onto a roller coaster. Massive rolling waves shoved their way down the narrow channel from the open seas beyond, angered by the sudden shallows of Nahwitti Bar at its mouth.

"Jesus, it's gonna be a rough ride out to the grounds. Hang on. You okay?" Paul quickly glanced over to see me already positioned like a sumo wrestler in the wheelhouse, feet apart and knees flexed, arms spread, hands clutching the dashboard. I knew all about keeping my balance and protecting my joints: stay loose, flexed, stable, and keep breathing, deep and slow. "I'm okay."

"It'll get better once we're over this fucking bar. We'll go straight out a couple of miles to where the shelf drops off at 50 fathoms, that's where feed gathers, and we'll turn west and start trolling along the edge. It's called the Yankee Spot and runs all along the top end of the Island. There's another fishing grounds about 12 miles offshore. Hey, did you take the coffee pot off the stove and put it in the sink? Okay, good. Anyway, that one is called the Steamer Grounds. The weather gets pretty wild out there and it's a long run in."

"So what can I do today?" I was relieved that at least there wasn't big wind along with the big waves, but the lowering gun-metal sky seemed to be preparing for some kind of assault.

"If the pilot holds out, you can come out to the stern and help lay out the gear in the cockpit, but I just want you to watch while I set out the gear and pull it in. You've got to know what you're doing back there or you can get into a hell of a mess and the gear is a fortune. One box of a dozen flashers is 57 bucks, and we can use 60 or 70 at a time."

"I've seen the bills. We've already spent almost $2,000 on gear. I'll be careful, I promise."

"When we get near the edge in a few minutes, I'm going to slow down to quarter-speed for trolling, about two or two and a half knots, depending on waves and current. You're going to keep the bow straight into the waves so we can be as stable as possible while I drop the poles. In heavy seas like this it can be very tricky, so we have to do this quick. When the stabies are in the water it'll be safe to turn the boat broadside to the waves. I'll come back in and set the pilot and hope the bloody thing works, and you can come out the stern and help me set gear. Okay . . . here we go. You ready? Get up on the seat here and take the wheel."

Heart pounding, I focused on riding straight into the looming swells. *I can do this. I can do this.* I would do my part to keep us safe while he did his.

It was very unusual to run with stabilizers unless it was deadly rough, as they slowed the boat down and ate up fuel with their heavy drag through the water. When trolling they were mandatory and settled down the boat considerably, not only with the 40-pound stabilizer boards in the water dragging on chains, but with the two 40-foot stabilizer poles, which were tied by ropes attached to cleats on the mast; they dropped the weight and centre of gravity down to about 45 degrees.

We had to let the stabilizers and their complex system of ropes and pulleys up and down by hand. They were so heavy I could let them out only by inching out the rope still wrapped once around the cleat, but I couldn't bring them up from the flattened position. If the rope got away from us, especially in rough waters, and if the pole dropped to the end of its ropes, we could tear up rigging and bust the bolts fixing it to the deck. We had to let them out smoothly and quickly, one after the other with just one of us or simultaneously if there were two of us, because just having the one side down destabilized the boat—especially dangerous in rough seas. If one set of ropes broke or tangled, we had to balance out with the other pole in the same position.

Typically you ran from your anchorage if you were pulled in for the night in sheltered waters or if you were tied up at a wharf. Usually you would go from anchorage straight out to the grounds, running with poles up, then slow down to trolling speed while still heading out, especially if you were nearing a whole grid pattern of boats trolling over a hot spot. If you had a good pilot, you would set it going straight out then lower your poles right away. If it was really rough, you slowed it down to half-speed because moving forward faster kept you more stable. If it was really, really rough, you always set the pilot straight into the waves, and if it was super rough, someone would have to steer into the waves—like now.

Paul quickly stepped aside as I flipped up the steering seat, braced myself against it and gripped the heavy wooden wheel. Never taking my eyes from the dark water crashing over our bow, I heard him grunt a final okay and the cabin door slam. Felt the whir and vibration of the rope running through the pulleys and knew Paul had started. I had done this before but not in such heavy seas, and when the boat lurched to one side as the pole and stabie went down, my heart kicked up a notch, waiting for the whir of the second rope. Any twist or knotting in the ropes would hang it up, and I knew enough to know that we would be in serious trouble. I rolled my shoulders and breathed deeper.

The clunk and splash and righting of the boat created an odd sensation of a slow-motion roller coaster and I thanked my genes again for my absence of nausea. Paul was back in the wheelhouse, pretty revved up.

"Okay, all done, you did great. Now get your rain gear on and go out to the stern and wait for me in the cockpit. Don't touch anything. It's pretty rolly, so be careful, especially getting into it—it's a long way down for you. I'm going to turn west onto the tack and set the pilot and keep an eye on it from the stern controls. There's hardly anybody out here to run into and we're pretty clear of pinnacles and reefs in this area. If the pilot fucks up you'll have to come back and steer."

It was rough and cold and miserable, but I was excited as hell getting into my shiny orange Helly Hansens. I already had on four layers of cotton and wool and leotards under my jeans and to that I added two pairs of grey wool work socks and black heavy-soled gumboots. The small-size bib overalls cinched tight and the hooded jacket had already been adjusted as much as possible to fit my 5-foot-3-inch self, with the bib ending up at my neck and the sleeves folded up twice. For now the trailing waste strap would wrap around me once. As I melted away over the months, it would wrap twice. The red toque I had crocheted for the trip completed the ensemble.

A cautious crab-walk got me to the stern in the heavy side-roll, where I carefully knelt on the lidded checkers (we would undoubtedly fill them with fish today) and slid down into the starboard side of the cockpit that I had decided would be my side. By then Paul had swung us into our westward tack and I watched the sullen, low shore slip by. Offshore there was an odd, dark density that seemed too low for clouds and too close for horizon.

I was grateful it had been so lovely the day before but sincerely hoped this bipolar spring weather would settle down soon. I had yet to learn that the North Coast never settled down and was as quixotic as the people were courageous.

"Okay, let's hope the pilot holds out. Jesus, you're in no danger of falling out." Paul laughed and took the lid off the wooden gearbox running along the back of the checkers. "You're up to your armpits in here. This is what you can do—get the gear ready for me. Remember how we stowed each rolled-up line of Perlon and lures and clipped it together with the snap? I want you to carefully unroll them by holding the snap and gently throwing the rest behind the boat to trail in the water, then snap it to the wire nailed across the cap rail. You have to make sure it's clipped on tight or you'll lose it and that's 5 or 10 bucks down the tubes. Line a few up and I'll start setting the gear."

"If I watch you set your side, can I set mine?"

"No, not today. You're always in such a rush to do things. Take it easy."

I knew it was pointless to insist. We worked together in concentrated silence as he explained how BC boats could drag six steel lines through the water, three on each side, weighted down with a lead cannonball weighing between 25 and 70 pounds. Ours were 40 pounds and stored in cup-shaped metal holders bolted to the side cap rail, a long reach from the cockpit when setting gear. Each 1/16-inch steel line of up to 150 fathoms (six feet to the fathom) was held on a hydraulic drum called a gurdy, three to a side, which played out one line to a system of bells and triggers spaced along the pole. The lines were submerged and set with gear one at a time, starting with the bowline, then the midline, then the *pig line*, so named because of the two-by-three-foot rectangular Styrofoam float attached at the line's midpoint, which caused it to swing out and keep the lines apart in the water.

As Paul slowly played out each steel line from the gurdy, its cannonball descended to a depth calculated by the number of sets of two metal beads fixed to the wire at one to three fathoms along the line. Each piece of gear was clipped between the two beads by its snap and gently trailed in the water, one after the other. When fully set, a troller resembled a butterfly above the water, while below, set 5 to 10 fathoms above bottom, it trailed scores of twirling lures that mimicked herring and the colourful, squidlike hoochies that were the spring salmon's dinner. The depth sounder in our cabin continuously flashed numbers that could mean bottom, fish, sunken wreck, reef, pinnacle or anything else its signal hit on the way down.

Bells on the stabilizer poles' rigging could signal a *smiley*, slang for a spring salmon over 12 pounds. But sometimes the bells didn't work and your fish got beat up by being dragged, or were eaten by seals, or if they weren't in season, died before you could shake them off. A good fisherman kept the gear moving up and down all day to simulate a school of feed, or feed ball moving in all directions, instead of just swimming in a straight line.

You pulled in the gear one line at a time so the other tow line kept fishing and to avoid a gear-tangling catastrophe. Normally, an experienced fisherman could go through all the gear, both sides, in a half-hour or so, but this session was a two-hour slow-mo' event as I absorbed every piece of action and instruction. The latest installment of Gear Setting 101 came rapid-fire but sequentially, and I vowed to myself that I would learn faster and more accurately than any other deckhand he'd had. I watched and nodded in profound, silent concentration. I relished the vertical learning curve, but I was restless for an action curve.

It was too rough and wet for me to write notes in my rapidly expanding *Sylvia's How-To Book* right then, but I would as soon as I could. I took notes as much as possible while Paul instructed and demonstrated. Some of the instructions became large-print bulletins that soon papered the cabin walls: *How To Start & Stop the Engine, How To Call A Coast Guard May Day, How To Light the Stove, How To Set the Pilot.* He delivered his calm, pedantic sessions like daily doses, prioritizing the must-knows, good-to-knows and maybe-later-knows. I mostly curbed my natural inclination to see and understand how everything fit together and tried to interrupt him only to check my notes and bullet-point lists with him. If not then, later in carefully chosen quiet times. Mistakes were costly in time, money and temper tantrums.

The odd grey wall I had noticed in the distance two hours ago seemed closer whenever I looked up from my marine classroom, and with a sigh Paul confirmed that it was one of the north end's infamous fogs. When the weather lowered, you had wind or you had fog. And this one was like something out of a Hollywood horror B-movie. I watched in shocked disbelief as it moved, eerily dense and soundless, across our deck to shroud us, then the water, then the land. We couldn't even see the pigs riding only 20 feet off our stern. Not an experience for a claustrophobic. Even I began to feel uneasy when I no longer saw land. The only thing we could still see were the six-foot waves still pounding our starboard side. Instinctually I became hyper-alert and spoke in whispers.

It was just as well the pilot broke down: I would have had to hand steer in the fog anyway, my eyes glued to the glowing radar sweeps that showed a vague representation of the coastline and, hopefully, other boats we might run into.

I kept one eye on the radar and the slowly thinning fog and another on a guide book to BC salmon I'd picked up at the Bull Harbour library. In the office, I learned the multiple names and life cycles of the fish I longed to get up close and personal with. I had heard so many different names I had to figure out which was what. It turned out each one had a Native name, a Canadian name, an American name and any number of nicknames.

All five species started out by hatching in the early spring in freshwater gravel stream beds up to 1,000 miles from the sea. They took from one to five years to travel downstream and through the ocean and then return to the exact spot they were hatched to lay and fertilize the next generation of eggs. The strangest part was that most of the species' males dramatically changed colour and even shape, growing fierce hooked jaws and humped scarlet backs to ward off competing males as they journeyed through the return of their cycle to spray their milt over the eggs in a nest the female had made by squirming in the gravel. After their struggle to reach their stream and emerge the alphas, the couple's mating was passionless and heralded a quick death.

In the royal court of Salmonry, the chinook was revered by the coastal First Nations as the king of salmon, the names it is known by in the US, though it is spring and smiley by current BC fishermen. They were the biggest, the showiest and the first to arrive on the fishing grounds. The early-season princely sockeyes, or *sox*, vied for the crown and won it: these second largest of fish became a focus when the much smaller cohos and pinks began to decline in the '70s. The average sockeye, which started running early in the season and could be taken with the springs, could bring in $10. A holdful of those beauties could make your whole season. Cohos, or small-sized blue-backs, were the dukes and couldn't be taken until July 1. The hefty chums, or dogs, were the servants of the court. Running late in the season and taken by net, they were destined for the canned market and institutional use. When canners wanted to glamour them up, they labelled them Fancy Keeta.

The lowly pinks—also known as humps, humpbacks or distasteful slimeballs—were small and hard to dress and worth pennies a pound, not considered worth a troller's time, and were left for the netters until they earned their new name in the early '80s: Desperation Fish. With runs of all the other species at record lows from 1980 to 1983, trollers would scramble for the pinks to save their season. No one knew just how bad it would get. Record-low runs and 18 percent interest rates, competing users and tightening restrictions on seasons and areas were moving in to form a crucible of their own.

For another three hours we rolled and bounced until the engine began to overheat again and about noon we had to pull in the gear, turn around and run back to Bull Harbour. We'd caught one 20-pound red spring that brought us $55 at the fish camp for five hours of rolling our guts out in the fog. At least we didn't come back skunked, but it was a grim ride back with Paul fuming about the Taylor Curse, which basically amounted to everything he touched turned to shit, according to him. There was nothing I could do to jolly him up, struggling with a bit of angst myself.

So what do you do when you're stuck on a boat and you have to *get away* before you come undone? Some people are adept at leaving *internally*: their spirit is elsewhere. It is certainly more efficient than having to leave physically. There are very few experiences more powerful and unnerving than trying to engage with someone who is so Teflon-coated that nothing sticks to them. Mighty handy for long periods on a boat, especially in isolation. Personal boundaries are a luxury, and so people go inward to find space. It is also free, instantaneous and infinite. But for those of us who are deeply engaged in the world and Velcro-skinned, detachment is illusive. What do we do? The irony of boat life is, though you're surrounded by limitless space, there's nowhere to go.

Paul and I were dying from constriction in the midst of endless space. I knew he was upset by all the boat problems, no fish and looming boat mortgage payments, but I had to get away from The Dungeon banging and didn't have anywhere to go but the 40-foot float.

I noticed the skiff was still tied to our midships cleat where Paul had used it to inspect the intake valves for obstructions, and

I got the brilliant idea to *get away* by rowing around the bay. I poked my head through the floor opening and told him my plan. He grunted in reply. I strapped on a life jacket and told our dock neighbour that I'd be rowing around. I knew better than to go out in the wilderness alone without taking precautions.

With every pull on the heavy wooden oars I felt lighter, like leaving the gravitational pull of some dark planet. I imagined myself as a water bug, skittering weightless across the surface, then a swan, gliding and elegant. It was so blessedly quiet and calm, the air so warm and gentle, and I couldn't tear my eyes from the ripple of my wake. My bones and tension softened like putty. I couldn't remember what I'd come out here to do and what had driven me here. My hands dozed in my lap as I drifted and drifted on the incoming tide.

It seemed the most natural and sensible thing to slide down onto my back. I knew I'd be perfectly safe in my gently rocking cradle, as certain as an infant, as I watched two eagles in a love dance high above me.

Suddenly, the silver blade of a jet bisected the sky. I smiled at this odd intrusion, smiled as the eagles' ballet continued in spite of it and wondered which was the greater miracle.

I breathed back into myself and patted my skin into place before rowing back across the silver bay. Our neighbour gave me a little wink and wave as I tied up the skiff and clambered back on board. He reminded me a little of my dad and I had the feeling he understood what I was doing drifting around the bay.

A few helping hands and sympathetic suggestions determined the engine alternator was the culprit this time, which meant another run down the channel to Hardy to get it fixed. With luck we would be fishing again in a couple of days. In the meantime I knew to lay low and keep myself occupied.

Un-Dressing Salmon

How do you dress a salmon? In fishnet stockings, of course.

Dressing a salmon is kind of a misnomer. Getting dressed usually means you add something to something—clothes to a person or sauce to a salad or stuffing to a turkey. But when it comes to salmon, you take things away: all their guts and gills.

With trolled salmon, it's not so much a disembowelling as it is a surgery. It is performed with as much skill and precision as a tossing deck will allow, because one false move costs you, literally. Any mark or cut or incorrect technique will downgrade the fish and you'll get paid a lot less for it. And when you're talking large red springs, the smileys, you're talking big loss. Not that we got much for our fish. By the time consumers buy it at the supermarket, everybody has taken their cut, so to speak.

Trolled salmon is the only fresh fish that is dressed before it's sold. They are caught on individual hooks, treated very gently and hygienically and preserved carefully in crushed ice 'til sold at a fish camp. Only second-grade fish are frozen, as the meat gets mushier when thawed.

Gillnet and seine boats catch their fish by net, and by the

time the fish are dragged in and dumped on deck or in the hold, the fish are pretty beaten up by their own frantic thrashing and being dragged through water en masse, mashed together and thrown around. Those poor carcasses go to the canning market, and, in worst case, become fertilizer or pet food.

The minute a troll-caught fish is pulled into the boat, it's dropped into wooden bins in front of the cockpit in the stern where you stand to pull in the gear. Hold the thrashing tail and hit the fish hard with a gaff or club, hopefully just once, where its neck would be if it had one. It is merciful and necessary, especially if it's a big spring. They are very strong and can create havoc, flinging other fish, gear and sometimes themselves in all directions, including overboard.

Unless there's a fish on every hook, which hasn't happened since Christ was a cowboy, wait 'til all the gear has been pulled, then dress the whole works at once. Sometimes it's a few, sometimes it's none.

After it is definitely dead (some people dress them when they're still slightly twitchy—a foolish and barbaric practice that wracks up some very nasty karma and results in lots of dressing injuries), prop the fish on its back in the four-foot V-shaped metal or wooden trough with the tail pointing toward your knife hand. Then the surgery begins.

Holding the head steady, with the thumb and forefinger of your other hand in the gills, insert the tip of the long, narrow, exceedingly sharp dressing-knife blade in the anus and make a smooth straight cut up to the throat, if it had one, stopping about an inch before the V-shaped patch where the bottom of the gills meets the throat. Reaching into the throat, cut away the membrane holding the entire gut ensemble.

If it's done right, you can grab the top of the membrane and pull out the whole business like opening a zipper and pitch it into a bucket. Pitching it overboard often costs you the dressing knife if you lose your grip. Undoubtedly there are a million pounds of stainless steel blades lying on the bottom of the ocean.

Inspect and dissect the internal organs later for personal interest or to see what goodies the fish have been eating and try to match the gear accordingly. Hours of scientific fun.

Next, cut the large blood vessel running along the spinal column and carefully scrape out all the congealed blood. Old blood is notorious for degrading the flesh. Then lift the gill flaps and with a circular motion cut through both sides at the same time if you're good, and one side at a time if you're not.

Then wash-wash, rub-rub with seawater pumped through the deck hose and the dressed beauty is ready for its icy bed in the hold.

The ice is snow cone textured and carried from the ice house through a large pipe containing a slowly turning auger. It's like a giant screw, carrying the ice at a steep angle up to a support beam on the edge of the loading dock, where it cascades down a multi-jointed pipe straight into the boat's hold. Someone had better be holding the end of it, directing the ice cascade into certain compartments. If not, you end up with a 2,000-pound snow cone in the middle of your hold that you can't do a thing with. You just have to shovel it out and start over.

If the ice is too chunky it won't fill the salmon bellies smoothly, making lumps and indentations that downgrade the fish. If it's too slushy, it'll melt in a couple of days and won't keep the fish fresh. You either end your trip early, losing money if the fishing is good, or take a risk and stay out, ending up with flattened funky fish that go for pet food.

The fish are laid in rows, each layer a different direction to evenly distribute the weight. The bellies are stuffed with ice to keep the meat fresh and the bodies from flattening and then laid neatly on their sides. Ice is packed around each fish and between each layer. People who don't bother with this step find the last couple of layers like salmon pancakes. The tricky thing is gauging how much ice to use on each layer so you don't run out too soon and have to come in.

The final layer is covered with an ice blanket made of some space age material. Imagine a multi-layered fish and ice cake.

Sounds like any old fool could pull this off, right? Think again. It is truly an art and a science with a million variables that reveal themselves through hard experience. The more care you take, the more money you get.

I wasn't a rookie at gutting fish, but we were catching so few springs that Paul wouldn't risk me messing up any of them while practising the exacting technique, especially when factoring in the pitching deck. We were into our fourth day of what we hoped would be a full 10-day trip since coming back from Port Hardy with the allegedly repaired alternator, trolling the Yankee Spot shelf from Goletas Channel across the whole top of Vancouver Island all the way to Fisherman Bay, which took a whole miserable day—13 or 14 hours of being thrown around in the pouring rain—then anchoring in Fisherman Bay or Shushartie Bay at the channel end, for two or three fish a day. At this rate, we were burning more fuel than we were earning to pay for it.

While scrounging around the camp store in Bull Harbour one day, I drifted into conversation with a well-seasoned skipper. Commiserating over my frustration at our poor catches, he passed on the sage advice an old Haida fisherman had given him years before when asked to share the secret of his success:

Be where the fish are.

"We were pissed off." He chuckled and shook his head over his youthful brashness. "We thought he would tell us about some hot fishing lures, but once we knew what was going on we realized that was true. For a good fisherman it's an instinctive thing. It's hard-wired somehow."

Instinct and a lot of knowledge, planning and good business sense—like any good entrepreneur. A highliner wasn't just about dropping your hooks in the water where the salmon were just dying to snap them up. The ocean was full of delectable goodies, and the fisherman's job was to figure out what would *lure* the fish in the right place at the right time to make that rubber and steel gizmo absolutely irresistible. Besides, it was a big ocean out there with lots of places to hide, and even when stocks were plentiful, they had particular habits and places to congregate for meals.

Salmon are picky eaters who enjoy a certain ambience, like specific temperatures and times of day and currents and tides. They are particularly fond of feed balls: dense clumps of herring and other creatures that provide an all-you-can-eat buffet, usually around reefs or drop-offs, where lunch likes to hang around in rocks and holes for protection.

Areas with a strong tidal flow are also great locations because baitfish are swept along with the current, making them an easy catch for the salmon. Salmon love breakfast and supper, so the morning and night bites are usually the most lucrative.

The best time to travel is with the current, when the tide is running strongest, because you want to be trolling during the slack tides, which last about an hour, just before the tide reverses. The feed fish come off the bottom because they don't have to fight the current, and when the salmon move in to feast, the troller makes most of his catch. Most of the time there are two fishable slack tides a day, but in summer there are occasionally days with three, which can really boost your catch.

The best time for fishing is when the moon is half full and tides are at a minimum. Tides are biggest around the full moon and new moon because they are affected by the moon's gravitational pull. And since fish have to spend most of their energy fighting big tides, they rarely feed, which means poor fishing.

You need to plan your tacks carefully so that you are on your hot spot at slack tide and do short tacks back and forth through the slack. A couple of miles off can make a huge difference, and if you overshoot your hot spot, or don't know about it, it can take ages to get back trolling at two knots an hour. That would certainly help explain why boats can be trolling at the same time in the same general area and some get skunked and some do well. Then there's the speed of the boat, the colour and shape and configuration of the gear, the motor sounds and vibrations, the astrological signs of the crew and some weird voodoo about the electrical current given off by the boat called the *bonding system*.

Apparently, fish are attracted to and repulsed by electrical currents and fields, and since every fishing boat creates an underwater field generated by its metals, steps must be taken to create just the right current to please salmon.

This is done by bonding or joining all metal components of a boat with a heavy electrical wire that is connected to underwater zinc bars attached to the boat's hull. Different metal objects in water create different currents, but when those objects are bonded, the currents are neutralized and a positive electrical field is created around the boat, 0.4 to 0.5 of a volt. After the boat is properly bonded, a *black box* can be attached to the steel trolling wires, sending electricity through the wire between 0.15 and 0.3 of a volt, depending on the boat's electrical field.

The voltage can be adjusted to attract different species and sizes of fish. The bigger the school and the smaller the fish, the higher the voltage they like.

We had zinced the hull but certainly didn't have one of those Star Trek black boxes. The maddening thing was we attracted hordes of small cohos anyway, which we had to shake off the barbless hooks because the season wouldn't open until July 1, just over a month away. And the only halibut or ling cod we could legally keep were dead on the line and destined for the fry pan. Originally, West Coast fishermen needed only one *A* licence to take any finned seafood, but in the '70s the *L* licence was created for bottom and flat fish like halibut and lings, and the *A* was retained for salmon. We could never sell *L* fish, but we sure could eat them. And there is nothing on this earth more delicious and life-giving than halibut or red snapper steaks just an hour out of the water. In fact, most fishermen prefer them to salmon.

It might have been thought easy enough to sneak a bunch on board, but the Coast Guard had collaborated with the Department of Fisheries in a new trolling fleet *boarding* program early that year whereby officials could legally inspect any boat for fishing infractions, even on the grounds, and if they found fish out of season or licence type, the boat would be escorted to the nearest town and the entire catch dumped, along with a hefty fine or even a tie-up period. We'd heard rumours that there had already been a couple of boardings and no one in their right mind would take a chance just in case a cutter came speeding up to their stern one day.

I had wanted the real deal and I was getting it. My alarm clock was the engine that started up behind my head. Getting up in the cold and dark at 5 a.m. after a few hours of restless sleep tossing at anchor was like swimming up through viscous dark water. By the end of the second day out, Paul allowed me to set a few pieces of gear and bring them in, unless I thought there was a salmon on the hook. Then insisted he be the one to clip the line to the stern and pull it in the six feet to the stern, where he expertly hit it on the back of the head with the gaff so he could slip the gaff under its gill and pull it over the stern and into the checkers. I could practise on the dead cohos or small *L* fish that were no financial threat if I lost them or accidentally cut into the belly flesh while dressing them.

I learned fast and never complained but yearned for a little tenderness and affection beyond the goodnight peck on the lips before descending to the fo'c'sle. We worked in silence most of the time and fell into our bunks exhausted at night, but I could feel every part of me building endurance and getting stronger with every day. So far, though, it seemed I was trading one set of worries and problems back home for another here. Despite all that, I loved being in this beautiful and perilous world and prayed the fishing would improve. Still, I daydreamed about having enough money to travel and go back to college for a nursing and counselling degree. I longed to see Paul's matinee-idol face free of thunderclouds.

Under the daily concerns that hit all the Big Buttons, like mortality and making a living, lurked the dark fear that my body couldn't take all I demanded of it out here, and I demanded a lot, maybe more than I should have. The issue of being a female in this male domain was already proven wrong every season by the few women in the fleet. My insistence to do more, be the best, was my Excalibur, my weapon against the memories of terrible weakness and pain. My dreams were still haunted by the sound of tearing metal and broken glass, the orthopaedic surgeon telling me I would never be what I had been; that I would be crippled by arthritis by the time I was 50.

I had ignored pain so long I had learned to almost deny its existence, but now I had to pay attention, because if something went really wrong, I was a long way from help. Sometimes I still let myself wonder if two years really was long enough for torn ligaments to reattach all along a spine, if it was all more than I could bear. I fought with bright bravado the fear, crouching dark and silent in the shadows, that I wouldn't make it through this time. That even if my body held out, the anxiety over money for school, the viability of this relationship and the barrage of divorce issues would take me down.

But no one who had watched that dark-eyed blondie stride around Hardy a couple of days earlier, taking photos of eagles prowling the mud flats, abandoned fishboats rotting in the shallows and silent First Nations women repairing nets, or chowing down in the town's *de rigueur* Chinese restaurant, or whooping it up with her honey and their hometown fishing friends at the raunchy Seagate and the Thunderbird, would ever know she had a care in the world.

Gaia's Whale

The mundane and the magical were such easy partners here. They slid in and out of the spotlight in perfect choreography, so smoothly I could hardly tell the difference, unless I was really paying attention. It was a little more work than dumbly plodding through the drama, but I never lost sight of how much magic was at work, and that more than made up for the effort. It suspended me above the brutishness and drudgery and terrors of this life. It was the kiss that made me smile in my sleep, the inner knowing that something so much greater was at play.

Mother Nature had another tantrum this day, or maybe it was a headache or indigestion. She huffed and heaved and bellowed and sent her house into chaos. It started out well enough for the north end, but as the day wore on she just couldn't resist having a hissy fit. Maybe sunny days made her cranky. By noon the winds were up to 20 knots and we were thrashing and grinding around the Yankee Spot with a few other hapless souls. We stayed because there was nowhere else to go. By all reports, everywhere else was just as windy and rough and fishless.

Some people didn't even bother to go out, figured they'd just end up spending more on fuel than what they took in and had themselves a harbour day. There was nothing more demoralizing than bashing around all day just to come back skunked, and there'd been an awful lot of that this season. But since we hadn't got skunked yet, we went out at daybreak.

The day before, I was so desperate not to come back to Bull Harbour empty-handed that I compulsively pulled my gear and swore I would not go back in until we caught something. Even Paul was relieved that we could finally run in when I pulled in a ratty little spring, a half-inch too short. Refusing defeat, I dressed the poor little thing, threw it on the deck and rolled on it like a dog, certain that would press the fish out to the minimum 16 inches for sale.

We were going into Bull Harbour for the night because we were worn out from tossing at anchor all night—even the bays were rough with harsh weather—and needed a decent sleep. And though I would never have asked to go in, I was relieved. As we ran down the channel from Nahwitti Bar I relaxed into the thought of a quiet night and peeled potatoes at the sink, watching for the harbour entry in the dense green shoreline. Suddenly the temperature gauge nearly blew off the dashboard and a horrible whine came up through the floor as we began losing power.

"Jesus Christ! Get up here and keep us steering straight. The tide is running in hard and will run us aground if we go broadside."

I leaped to the wheel, heart pounding. Paul ripped up the carpet and floor cover and threw them on the day bunk. Choking steam belched up as the emergency lights and alarm turned the engine room into a scene from Dante's inferno.

"God, Paul, be careful," I shouted above the din and my adrenaline.

"Turn off the engine and turn on the radio telephone to the Bull Harbour frequency. If I can't get restarted we're going to need help." He grabbed an extra extinguisher from the cabin wall and jumped down into the engine room.

As I wrestled with the wheel to keep our rudder straight, I said my first prayer of the season through trembling lips and willed us away from the rocky shorelines that loomed on either side of this treacherous little channel. I gripped the wheel so hard my hands turned white. I flashed back to all the whitewater canoeing accidents I'd survived and reasoned that at least I was still in a boat and not in the icy water.

For once I was relieved to hear Paul banging and swearing because I knew he was still alive down there, and I stopped myself from calling out to him, gauging our danger level by the intensity of the tirade. *Come on, Paul, you can do it, you can do it,* I murmured over and over. Suddenly he was in the wheel-house, pouring sweat and gunk, and as he pulled me off the seat, he grabbed the wheel and turned the key on the dashboard. Click. Click. Click. Click. Then the most beautiful sound in the world: the roar of a diesel. I threw my arms around his waist and hugged him as he pulled the boat around to head back up the channel to harbour.

"Hey, take it easy, you'll get this crap all over yourself," he said, and put his arm around my shoulders for a quick squeeze and a crooked smile. He was cavalier but I could see his pulse still pounding in his throat. "You did good. It's that fucking alternator again. I'm gonna kill that guy in Hardy. He guaranteed it was fixed. But I think it's okay now. I'll work on it more when we get in, then we'll get a shower."

Back in Bull Harbour, the camp manager watched me pull that flat little scrap of a fish out of the checkers and throw it on the scale and discreetly eyed my grease-covered clothes. He quietly marked it on my fish slip and paid me the few bucks it wasn't really worth as if I had hauled out a whale. I wouldn't have been surprised if it went to crab bait, as he hadn't the heart to refuse it in front of my flat little scrap of a self.

After a bit more banging and swearing in the engine room and a lot of commiserating with the Bull Harbour Boys, Dan appeared with a used alternator he kept as a spare that was compatible with our engine. He waved away the last few dollars from our money jar and said it was just a loan and he would catch us later for it. "We can't have you and your sweetheart losing any more fishing time than you have to," Dan said, in his soft drawl and kind smile. And it was his kindness that broke through my resolve and brought the tears that were never shed in danger.

We sold our few fish that afternoon—$194 for four gruelling days—and topped up our fuel and ice to establish our right to use the camp's laundry room and showers. In the cramped metal shower stall, under the steaming powerful jets, we made love like wildcats, oblivious to the rhythmic metallic banging that carried out over the camp through the open window. We were alive and proving it.

But hell hath no fury like a fisherwoman skunked.

And skunked we were the next day, as we bashed it out on the tacks 'til dinnertime and limped into Fisherman Bay to anchor for the night. The marine report said it would blow southeast the following day, so the north end would be somewhat sheltered and we could just troll back across the Yankee Spot to Bull Harbour. For now it was quiet, the hissy fit appeased. That was typical for a nor'wester: quiet mornings and nights, but screaming all day. Brilliant sun but icy-cold wind, like a glacier exhaling on you.

We'd managed to pull in a couple of rats, what the salty dogs called skinny, barely regulation-length salmon, and a glorious red snapper that we wolfed down for dinner. And puttered around the cabin, cleared and cleaned and relished the silence.

It doesn't register how irritating the droning grind of the engine is until it shuts off and then you realize how much energy you use to ignore something, especially something as penetrating and enormous as boat machinery and weather noise. I guess our brains have to numb to it or we'd go berserk. Some people replace it with blasting music or radio telephone talk, but for us, then, silence was a mercy.

As Paul dozed on the day bunk, I filled the tiny sink and dishpan with water heated on the oil stove and performed the art of dishwashing in less water than it took to run a cold glass of water at home—and that included rinsing. As I started the process, as careful and precise as a Japanese tea ceremony, my eyes lifted to the tiny window. I often wished the windows in the old tub were bigger; I also knew that showy windows were deadly when a freak wave slammed into your side. They popped out like contact lenses and the cabin filled up like a bucket.

So I had to be satisfied with this sturdy little peephole. It was an odd view, slowly swinging in an arc, sweeping back and forth as the powerful tides swung the boat at the end of its tether. It was like seeing the world through a camera lens. I fancied that the gentle movement was Gaia herself, dozing and calm for once in the amber light of sunset. Sweep to the right—luminous sandy crescent trimmed in dense furry green. Sweep to the left—silvery mirror reflecting the pearls and violets of an abalone shell.

Breathing in, breathing out, there was nowhere and nothing more than this. Breathing in, breathing out, water lapped and gurgled at our hull. Breathing in, breathing out, my hands moved like skilful fish in the soapy warm sea. There was nothing and nowhere more than this.

A powerful whoosh filled the air and I wondered if Gaia was snorting in her sleep. Nothing seemed too outlandish anymore. We swung to the left and I saw tiny concentric rings moving outward from a circular depression in the water. Then all was still again. I wondered if I had just imagined it. We swung to the right and again the mighty whoosh. It was such a benign sound but somehow immense and mighty at the same time. I had nothing to compare it to and my curiosity demanded an explanation, no matter how odd or even frightening.

I glided out onto the deck just in time to see a towering V-shape slide vertically back into the water, not more than 20 feet from me. My mind leapt to explain this stunning sight and came up with one option: whale. From the size of his flukes he must have been unimaginably huge, and I was acutely aware of how tiny and isolated we were. I flailed through my memory file for reports of whale attacks and found nothing. I prayed that the benign tales of these gentle giants were true.

There was an odd bulging in the water, as if there just wasn't enough room down there for whatever it was and the water too. The bulge became a dark grey mound rolling on and on just above the surface. Suddenly, a rubbery hole, like a giant belly button, appeared, dilated and sent up a fountain of fine spray. It may not have been Gaia exhaling, but it was something just as miraculous.

The whale must have been preparing to dive, because miles later his tail slowly lifted from the water and paused before sliding back down in perfect and graceful slow motion. It towered over us like Atlantis sinking, with hardly a ripple or sound to mark its path. I wondered if experiences like this were what helped to fuel that legend. He may have known that a few good swipes with that tail would shatter us. He may have chosen not to. He may have been too evolved to indulge in destruction just because he could.

Turned out this fellow was a regular fisherman too, coming into this bay with the incoming tide most nights to catch his supper. I was amused that the whale's cuisine was miniscule brine shrimp and krill when humans killed any old damn thing they could—the bigger the better. Made me wonder who the true monarch was, who really invented *noblesse oblige*. My bet was on the humpback. I filled myself up with the thrill of that rolling mountain and towering tail a few more times, wished him good fishing and then went back inside to finish the dishes.

Every time we were in this bay at sunset when the tide was moved in, I watched for him. I told him how beautiful and wonderful he was and apologized for all the awful things people have done to his relatives. I thanked him for his gentleness and asked him to be patient with us a while longer. We were still a foolish and juvenile species, I believed, though with lots of potential; he and his kind were the sighing grandparents who still loved us, no matter how naughty we were.

Maybe that's why the whales returned to the sea so many millennia ago. Maybe they just wanted to leave town before the kids moved in—kind of like retiring to Florida.

Davy Jones's Locker

If the most beautiful sound in this world is a dead diesel engine growling back to life while your boat is hurtling down a narrow channel in a ripping tide, then the most horrific sound is steel lines snapping and the whir of them whipping through the air. Things seem to sneak up on you out here, often when you least expect them, when you let your hyper-vigilance slip for just a moment. If you didn't start in this business with all six senses at full-on radar, you honed them quickly and efficiently, often the hard way. Those who didn't slipped away.

After three weeks, I had finally proved myself capable of setting and pulling gear on my own, gradually building up to several sets a day, and was powerfully proud to have claimed the starboard side of the cockpit as mine. My Viking heart sang as I worked silently alongside my mate in the wind and rain and rough seas, completely present, completely focused and aware—like in meditation, like in the Be Here Now mantra of the Eastern religions I read about at night or when I had to steer. Was it a coincidence I had found the *Three Ways of Asian Wisdom* in the Campbell River bookstore? Somehow I didn't think so.

Sometimes anchored at night I would share the occasional line or paragraph while Paul puttered, and I'd get a rare glimpse into his kaleidoscopic inner world: his world travels, wickedly funny mimicry, fractured childhood, art school degree, two estranged children in California only a decade younger than me.

I was just thanking the sea gods for our first relatively calm but drizzly day when the boat suddenly heaved to starboard. My immediate thought was that a queer wave had shoved us over, but we continued to list and started to veer. I froze in the few seconds of silence before Paul's mighty "Fuuuuuck!" signalled the maelstrom.

"Jesus, Paul, what's happening?" I knew enough to slam my gurdy lever to the OFF position to stop the line I was setting from spooling out. I had no idea what to do and watched, horrified, as we heeled over further. The entire boat seemed to be straining and I felt like I'd been flung into a nightmare.

"Stay down in the cockpit. We're caught on something and I have to stop the engine or the lines will snap and we'll lose our gear."

While he wrestled with the engine's stern controls, the steel lines snapped one after the other and whipped through the air from the tremendous force of their release underwater. We could do nothing but crouch in the cockpit until the devastation was over and the broken lines lay sprawled on the deck. Thank God we were still moving and Paul's side seemed to be okay; he was already striding around the deck beside himself.

"I've trolled over this area a million times and never had this happen. We've lost half our fucking gear. Maybe if you'd been in the wheelhouse steering instead of depending on this lousy pilot and watching the sonar this wouldn't have happened. Maybe we went off course."

I strode into the cabin, trembling from shock and adrenaline and the growing realization of how much money we'd just lost, and checked the pilot and sonar.

"We're still on tack and there is nothing on the sonar. What do we do now?" I felt my resolve to be calm and supportive weaken as he flung a chart to the cabin floor and barked "Move" as he stormed back out to the deck. I took a couple of deep, trembly breaths to calm my pounding heart and followed him out. I was not a yeller and did not want to start now. I had to live with this man on this boat and knew if I let things slide, it could get intolerable, yet I wasn't going to give up. I still clung to my lifelong habit of going quiet or getting weepy in a fight. What would happen when I didn't? I had an incredibly long Nordic fuse, but under these surreal circumstances, one of these days it might just get lit, and that scared me just about as much as his tirades.

"We're almost at Nahwitti, so what the hell, we might as well keep trolling with the one side until we get there. Can't afford the fuel to run and who knows? We may even catch a fish," Paul sniped, and kicked the wash-down bucket on his way to the cockpit. "I don't know what you're going to do, but I'm going to check to see if we have enough line left on the gurdies to limp along with the two spare cannonballs I've got in the hold. Won't make much difference using only five lines; there's no goddamn fish anyway."

"Okay, I'll make lunch. How about that little coho that came in dead? I've already got it baking in the oven and I can make up sandwiches."

"I don't care," he barked, and started to yank on the loose ends of the wire on the deck.

My concession to bad temper was a hard pull on the cabin

door and the satisfying slam behind me that punctuated my return to the cabin. I stood in the wheelhouse and slowly scanned the misty shore and long swells that rolled toward it. I breathed and breathed until my heart slowed and my hunched shoulders sank. I went to reach for a cigarette but remembered we'd smoked our last yesterday. Well, that certainly didn't help our twangy nerves.

After my requisite self-pep talk, I gave myself up to the comforting and primitive simplicity of making food and tending to the cave, which included the critically important House Rule Number One: No Rain Gear or Boots In the House. I cringed every time I saw fishermen schlep in and out of their cabin in full regalia. Those were the true *salty dogs*. The inside of their cabins was barely distinguishable from the deck or the engine room, or in extreme cases, the fish hold. Sometimes it looked like all three. I had been politely invited by these kind-hearted fellas to sit where slime-covered gear was just pushed aside; graciously offered coffee from cups plucked from piles of engine parts on galley counters black with grease and engine oil. And I would just as graciously refuse, even if psychotic from caffeine withdrawal. Fortunately, these were the exceptions, not the rule, and one of the reasons female deckhands were so highly prized. Only the most feral of women would tolerate living in a bacterial science experiment.

But even with the House Rule and a natural inclination to the clean and tidy, I had never been so dirty . . . and wet. I'd almost forgotten what dry and clean felt like. In my damp shelf of a bunk I was acutely aware from the wave sounds that the only thing separating me from total submersion was the wooden plank wall. Once that very wood was damp and breathing and permeable itself, so why would it be dry now? Even on those rare sunny days, I was either wet with sweat from physical labour on a fishing day, or I baked in the sheltered ovens of tiny bays and inlets, where the frigid northwest wind that brought the sun couldn't find you.

Life on a boat in the water means you are always wet. It ranges from moist to sodden. Even when you're in bed, you're not dry. And why should you be? In this climate, the elements of air and water are more related than usual. Even when it's numbingly cold, you sweat under your layers and rubber. And if you aren't wearing cotton or wool and you haven't bathed for a week or two, the aroma that wafts from some of those salty dogs is deadlier than mustard gas.

Here was the irony: while we wallowed in more water than we ever wanted to see and were damper than anyone was meant to be, there was no water to wash in. Every drop of fresh water was precious. We had one water tank in the hold that was filled at the fish camp and that had to last us for days . . . and days. As we grew mouldy with wet, we lived in drought conditions. *Water water everywhere but ne're a drop to drink.* We were soaked to the skin and dehydrated at the same time.

Being female presented an even greater challenge, feminine hygiene not to be confused with salty dog hygiene. A bath became a quart of water. A tub or shower became a metal hand basin the size of a salad bowl, set aside carefully so it wouldn't be used for anything else, like a salad bowl. If I could have reached, I swear I would have licked myself clean like a cat. But since I couldn't, I took a birdbath every night by the measly heat of the miserly oil stove and slipped into my comforting flannelette nightie and woolly socks. Paul said it made me look like a granny. I said I didn't care, but it hurt me, just a little.

Hair was a particular challenge. Not only was my hair oily,

but crusty too. Salt water became my gel and hairspray and high-lighter kit. Either you have little-boy hair that becomes a Mohawk in three days or you bind and gag longer hair in braids welded to your head. Don't even think about the windblown sex-kitten look. At the very least you will look like Popeye's Sea Hag, and at the worst, airborne hooks and gear will catch in it, or it will tangle in whirring machinery and rip your damned scalp off.

When it came to personal hygiene at sea, torrential rain was my best friend. As it poured off the roof I collected it in every cook pot and basin we had (buckets were reserved for guts and sea water). The trick was to keep the water in them until the sun came out—nature's blow-dryer. Timing was everything. Housekeeping tip: shampooing your hair on deck also helps wash the slime away! Take note, Martha Stewart. Unfortunately, this method required a second set of hands to slowly pour the rainwater over my head. If the sun was coming out any time soon and extra hands weren't available, I knelt just inside the cabin and draped myself over the raised doorway—waist height was just right for balancing. Then I poured cups of water over my dangling head with one hand as I worked the suds out with the other. Since there was mostly no sun, I had to remember to crank up the heater before the procedure (if we weren't low on fuel) so I could thaw my frozen scalp and not die of pneumonia. Things dried very slowly, if at all, especially hair. Some people opted out of all this and just put up with crusty, smelly hair 'til they got to a fish camp and a hot shower.

The fish camp shower was one of God's tender mercies. There seemed no end to this bounty of fresh water. Scalding and powerful, the torrent kneaded my knots and soothed my twangy nerves 'til I was stuporous. If there was only one stall at whatever camp we were in and I had to follow after one of the salty dogs,

I just bleached and scrubbed my way in. Centuries later, after losing five pounds of skin and grime, I'd stagger out limp and blessedly dry, pink and rubbery as a kewpie doll, except for my fisherman's tan, my hair dancing about my head and shoulders, a shade lighter than the last time.

While I was being laundered, so (usually) were our clothes in the camp coin machines, normally beside the shower. And when I and the laundry were done, I'd scrub and clean the cabin while Paul scrubbed and cleaned the hold.

On this day, I dragged the carpets off the linoleum, slung them over the boom and beat them to within an inch of their lives with a gaffing club, not only in my relentless efforts to remain hygienically civilized, but to blow off some steam. When I glanced over at Paul hunched over the gurdies and wire, I saw his wry half-smile.

"Something funny?" I flung over my shoulder, swinging for all I was worth.

"I'm just glad that's not me on the receiving end of that gaff."

"Humph."

"Hey look, I'm sorry." He clambered over the wire he was attaching to the cannonballs. "I was being a real asshole taking my frustrations out on you. It wasn't your fault and God knows you're hard enough on yourself trying to get everything right. Jesus, it'll probably be me that drives you nuts, not the fishing."

Tears welled up. I couldn't trust myself to speak, and let the gaff drop to my side. The last thing I'd expected was this much conflict between us. I could stand anything but that, after the end of my marriage less than two years ago and the pitiless divorce and husband I was still not free of.

"Look, if I ever yell at you like that again, you can kick me in the ass. Okay?"

"What?" I burst out laughing through the lump in my throat. "Are you crazy? I can't do that."

"I'm serious. I deserve it for being such a jerk. Okay, how about this. We'll be in Bull Harbour soon and I'll buy some more flashers and Perlon on credit. It's going to be a sunny afternoon, so how about we take your salmon sandwiches and go around the corner from the camp to an old Indian village site I heard of and look around for a while? Then I can just finish up this stuff tonight. Just put down that gaff, okay? I don't want to end up in Davy Jones's locker." He chuckled and flashed his gigolo smile.

Just before the Nahwitti Bar, we noticed a distinctive orange hull anchored by itself in a small bay. Paul radioed on the short-range Mickey Mouse, hoping it was our friend Gerry from False Creek. He was just about to give up when Gerry's unmistakable Kris Kringle voice broke in. He and his six-year-old son, Peter, and his deckhand, Mike, had just arrived at the top end and were anchored up getting ready to start fishing the next day. When he heard of our gear disaster, he graciously offered to *lend* us one of his spare cannonballs so we could fish with all six lines. He'd heard the fishing was slow everywhere and likely knew we were broke from scratching around for the last five weeks and couldn't afford the cannonball, the most expensive part of trolling gear. We decided that after our little exploration trip and buying more regular gear (on account) in Bull Harbour, we would run back out to tie up with Gerry in the bay that night.

"Hey. How would you like to go straight to the old village site now and have lunch? Looks like it's clearing up a bit and it'll be nice there." Paul glanced over at me refolding and stowing charts in the wheelhouse and pushed the throttle forward to pick up speed after the choppy bar.

"That would be great. I'd love that," I said, stepping over to smile up at him. "What about the gear?"

"We can pick it up on our way back out to tie up with Gerry in the bay. We have to get it on credit, so I'd rather be there around dinnertime when there won't be so many people in the store. Jesus, it's embarrassing." His face darkened. "What the hell. Let's go explore. I've heard you can still find some beads. Pack up our lunch and get ready. It's just a few minutes away around the bottom end of Hope Island here."

We anchored in the idyllic little bay and rowed to a perfect white crescent beach rising to a grassy knoll bordered by salmonberry bushes, trembling aspens and towering pines. Remnants of a wooden two-storey house set back in the trees and stunted corner posts on the knoll were all that was left of the Native people's village. But the graffiti of carved names and painted *We been here* and carpet of smashed booze bottles revealed later visitors.

We stood in front of the tumbledown front door. "Imagine seeing this out your front door," I said, looking out over the glittering bay and islands dotting the channel. "It's paradise. Everything you could want is here. Look at the next little cove. I can see the gorgeous colours in the tide pools from here. And look at the size of the mussel shells. I've never seen them so huge. Let's go down there."

"And all some people want to do is come here and wreck it. Look at all this garbage. What a bloody shame. Maybe we can find some beads for you. I know you love that kind of stuff." Paul scuffed at the mossy soil and glass shards.

"No, it's okay. I don't feel right about it. Let's just leave things alone." I felt a heaviness in my chest and took a deep breath to lift the sudden pall. The rising tide had already covered much of the beach, so we clambered along the rocky shoreline, carefully avoiding the brilliant kaleidoscope of sea life.

"Paul, look at those anemones. They look like emerald-green broccoli standing up in a grocery bin and as soon as they sense us coming they pop into themselves. Now they look like St. Patrick's Day doughnuts with chocolate centres."

"Wow, they do. They're making me hungry. How about one of those sandwiches out of your kangaroo pouch?" He gave the bulging front of my yellow anorak a playful poke.

"Once we eat our sandwiches, let's gather some of those giant mussels on the rocks for dinner tonight with the boys. They've got to be six inches long. I'll use this aluminum foil and sandwich bags to put them in, and carry them in my front pocket back to the boat."

"Okay, pioneer girl, let's go hunt down dinner." Paul smiled and brushed the mop of sun-streaked hair from my eyes.

After we filled my pocket with mussels, I allowed myself one treasure to mark this astounding day—an exquisite abalone shell with vivid pearlescence that I'd found near the knoll. I whispered my gratitude as I held it to my chest.

When we returned to Bull Harbour camp, I asked Anne, the first aider/accountant, if she knew anything about the old village site. Her grey eyes went stormy.

"That site has been horribly ravaged by non-Natives doing so-called digs, including using bulldozers," she said, her mouth going hard as she turned my shell over and over in her hands. "They sell everything they can find, including little beads—disgusting. They're no better than the European traders that came here 200 years ago. They're still ripping off the Natives and can't even leave that old site in peace."

As I turned to join Paul hurrying to the boat, I suddenly

mentioned we had gathered mussels from the rocks for our dinner.

"Honey, I wouldn't eat those if I were you. Dump them overboard." Anne pointed to a bulletin tacked to the corkboard in the office. "There is a possible red tide and they might be contaminated. Fisheries was here taking samples two days ago and gave us this notice to post. Didn't you hear it on the Coast Guard radio? They will issue a report in a couple of weeks. In the meantime, don't eat any shellfish from the north end. It could be deadly. The red tide is like clouds of toxic bacteria that just comes out of nowhere and contaminates shellfish. It's deadly to humans and takes weeks for the shellfish to flush out in the sea water. Promise me you'll throw that stuff overboard."

I solemnly promised and hugged her goodbye in gratitude. Paul watched dumbfounded as I poured the bucketful of mussels and sea water overboard and told him why.

"Jesus, we really dodged a bullet on that one," Paul said. "Good thing you told her. They don't know for sure yet, so maybe they were okay. Oh well. C'mon, let's get untied and get out to meet Gerry while it's still light enough for repairs."

After rounds of handshakes and hugs, Gerry and Mike helped Paul restring the steel wire and make up more gear lines while I cooked us up a feast—spaghetti and halibut steaks.

We were poor as peasants but ate like royalty on the gifts the sea provided: salmon, red snapper, halibut, ling cod and the occasional crab or smoked salmon shared by our Bull Harbour neighbours. All that high-end protein and omega-3s along with the porridge and potatoes and brown rice created a high-octane fuel that powered us through 16-hour days and honed our bodies to bone and muscle. I was connecting deeply with my body again, trusting in its strength and agility. No matter what happened over the next three months, that recovery was worth everything. I was becoming me again.

And later that night, as I stepped out on our deck to bring in the bag of fresh fruit Gerry had surprised us with, I turned a slow circle, arms outstretched to the tangy air and fiery sunset, the silent dark forest, the two old wood boats bobbing together companionably, the light from our cabin full of savoury smells and cigarette smoke and laughter, and filled myself up with it.

Salmon Prince

There was nothing I wouldn't do. I would turn myself inside out to prove I could do it. Anything. I was fierce: a lioness padding around my 39-foot territory. *Bring it on*, I snarled. *Think I'm too girly? Bring it on. Think I'm too little? Bring it on. Think I'm too citified? Bring it on.* I could sleep less, eat less, learn faster, make fewer mistakes and be more cheerful than any deckhand in this fleet. And when Paul told me not to, because it was too heavy or too dangerous, I'd wait 'til he was napping or distracted and then I'd do it anyway, and find a better way to do it.

It was a rare and glorious day of oily smooth seas, caressing breeze, benign sun and all the world rejoiced—at least, this part of it did. Those were the days so full of God's grace, when Gaia was her most loving and tender and I couldn't imagine being anywhere or doing anything else.

There'd been nothing on the lines for the last two pulls and there wasn't another boat for miles. We'd scrubbed and organized, repaired and patched, tied more gear and checked the glistening beauties lined up in their chilly beds like dollars in the till, their gutted bellies chubby with crushed ice in the hold.

I was secretly thrilled when Paul announced he was hitting the bunk for a nap. The autopilot was working for once and all I had to do was keep an eye on things. "Don't get yourself into trouble," he said, reminding me he wouldn't hear me through sleep and the engine's thrumming.

We were trolling our way back to Bull Harbour and that would take hours. I was so excited it was hard to act nonchalant. I felt like a kid left at home alone and I was going to do everything. Alone. I was going to catch a Salmon Prince.

I'd surprise him. When he woke up, I'd wait 'til he staggered out on the deck, blinking and yawning, glancing around for evidence of my folly. He'd see none. I'd pretend to be bored and make small talk. Then I'd casually mention that something got left behind the last time we dressed and iced the fish. He'd sigh and bitch about dried-up fish and lost money and yank the bin cover off. And there my prize would be. Huge. Perfect. Magnificent. And worth three days of groceries. Paul would never interfere with the fish on my side again and I'd pull in my own damn smileys. And I would smile and smile, just like the name intended me to do.

I took a deep breath and climbed into my Hellys and gumboots and cinched them good and tight. I did an all-points check, walked carefully along the deck and eased myself into the cockpit. No vaulting—hard to pull in a smiley if you're lying in the cockpit with a broken leg. One more scan and a prayer to the Salmon Spirits. I checked the gear, his side first. I *willed* everything into silence. If he woke up it would ruin everything.

The usual pull-pull, grab-throw of the gear, elevated to a

martial art: be the motor lever, be the spinning gurdy, the steel line, the clips, hoochies and hooks, the flashers, swivels and leads. But there was only a little drowned sockeye, which I set aside for the oven, and a couple of brown bombers, the pesky local rock cod, which I graciously unhooked and released. Undaunted, I knew my prize, my Salmon Prince, awaited me on my side of the boat—the good side.

I paused to scan around us again. No point making a big score if someone ran into the boat 20 miles offshore. The time was nigh and I moved to the magic side.

Bow cable: nothing. Main cable: nothing. How could 30 gear lines be empty? Pig cable: I counted down 10 lines, only 5 more to go. If they were empty, I would lose my chance. Paul would be awake before the next pull. *Please, please, please be there.*

And on the 14th line, the Salmon Prince.

I felt him before I saw him, a slight thrumming tension as I unclipped the Perlon from the line. Re-clipping it, I nudged the motor lever forward to stop the cable from spooling onto the gurdy drum. My heart kicked up a notch as I whispered instructions and encouragements to myself: "If you don't secure the line he could yank it out of your hands. Don't jerk the line or make sudden noises, or he'll bolt. If he's not hooked hard, he'll jerk his head and pull the hook out."

With both hands I transferred the clip to the holding wire on the inside edge of the stern. I breathed deep and eased into stillness, utterly focused. The world telescoped down to a scarred wooden ledge, a Perlon line and five feet of silky water.

I seduced the line in, hand over hand, a few inches at a time. The surface of the water bulged slightly and there was his dark back fin and, miles behind, the tip of his tail, languidly sweeping from side to side. I drew him to the stern, transfixed by his muscular, graceful beauty. He showed me first one side, then the other. *Am I not exquisite?* he said. *Am I not a miracle of perfection?*

I understood why the ancients sang songs of love and gratitude to the plant and animal beings around them. I understood why they asked permission to take lives that sustained their own, why they performed rituals of gratitude and humility. It wasn't just to ensure future plenty but to honour their partners in the dance of life and death.

I felt my heart swell with joy and the cooling tracks of tears on my face. Shaking, I reached for the spiked gaff. He was too massive to pull in by the line. The hook had pierced just inside the corner of his mouth. Even if the hook held, the line would slice my hands open hauling him in. My only chance was to hit him precisely behind his head with the club side of the gaff to stun him so I could haul him over the stern by the hook side.

I brought the gaff down and missed. He swam gently. I hit again and missed. By then I was weeping. He continued swimming gently. "Please help me, I don't know how to get you in," I whispered. My civilized mind recognized the madness in this, but it came from a great distance. I couldn't bear to club him again, to submit him to my clumsy attempts.

This time I reached down as far as the waist-high stern would allow. Balanced on the transom, I tipped forward and slipped the gaff hook under his gill. What madness was this? One lurch and I would launch headfirst into the chuck to be his briny bride forever. But he held steady and leaned gently to his other side. I wondered if I was just dreaming.

"I'm going to pull you into the boat now," I crooned. Easing back to the floor, I started to haul him out of the water. He was impossibly heavy and I was too short to get the leverage I needed. I grunted and strained and begged him not to thrash, begged every deity I knew and some I didn't to help me. I was shaking with tension and wondered how long he would tolerate dangling in another element. Paul had lost a monster spring the day before. Just as he was pulling it over the ledge by the gaff the fish freed itself with a mighty twist and flung itself back into the water. In my other life I would have cheered it on, but we were so damned broke I cursed its freedom. It felt like someone had opened my wallet and torn up the money in front of my face, or stolen my food and shoes.

The Prince's head appeared at the stern ledge and I crouched lower, straining every muscle in my body. The ocean and I had given birth to this beautiful slimy creature and with one more grunting cry he slithered over the stern and into the cockpit, where he slowly flapped and gasped. I couldn't bear to see him drowning and struggled to lift him into the bin, cradled in my arms. I stroked his luminous flank once, thanked him for the gift of himself and then hit him hard, precisely behind his head.

When Paul stumbled out onto the deck, blinking and yawning, he glanced around for signs of my folly. Instead, he found me sitting quietly on the hatch cover, gazing at the hazy line of land.

I was too tired to lift my prize into the dressing tray—he did. He didn't insist on dressing him—I did.

He took a photo of me in my Helly Hansens and gumboots. I braced the Prince against me, hands in gills, knees bent from the weight. His nose was at my heart, his tail at my knees. He was as wide as my body was thick.

Bob, the camp manager, weighed him in at 52 pounds and called everybody down: his wife, Marji, Anne the first aider/ accountant, his son-in-law, Mike, and the two summer boys who were shovelling ice and packing fish on the wharf—all the folks who were becoming like family. My Prince was the best they'd seen so far that year. The admiring nods and incredulous stares of the camp staff and other fishermen who wandered over to find out what the fuss was all about made everything worthwhile: the worrying, the weariness, the bangs and cuts, the raw wounds.

My hands took the worst of it. Every morning an agony. I had to flex to get them moving, and the sores that had dried up overnight, thanks to my spectacular immune system, cracked open and bled. Problem was, we just couldn't find industrial-strength rubber gloves to fit. When the gloves slid back and forth, especially when I dressed fish, I struggled just to keep the damn things on. I even tried wearing an old pair of wool gloves inside the rubber gloves, but that was like trying to do surgery in oven mitts. Then I tried duct-taping the gloves on, but that just took the skin off my forearms. Since I constantly handled rough or pointy objects and razor-sharp knives on the pitching deck of a boat—much like preparing Christmas dinner while your house is spinning in a tornado—my hands were a roadmap of injuries. So I went gloveless and prayed I wouldn't get blood poisoning.

Apparently, fish slime is particularly toxic to humans when introduced by knife cut and can send susceptible people off to the closest hospital, hopefully faster than the blue line of poisoning creeping up their arms. I never did get blood poisoning, but I did get the dreaded Fish Bite. It doesn't kill you, but it hurts so much you wish it would. It comes from fish slime rubbing on your hands, particularly with loose gloves, and eats away your skin like battery acid. Next thing you know, you've got raw weeping patches between your fingers that are damn near impossible to heal in dirty, wet conditions. The longer you ignore them, the worse they get, until your hands feel like they've been caught in a leghold trap and you just want to chew them off.

While Paul was unloading the couple of handfuls of fish, I stripped off my rain gear and went down to the fo'c'sle to change for the usual laundry-and-shower extravaganza. Even without a mirror, I was shocked to see the state of my thinning body, besides my emerging ribs and hip bones. The light from the little skylight in the fo'c'sle roof revealed so many bruises I looked like the Tattooed Lady at the county fair. My body was an illustrated account of every collision with something much harder than myself over the last five weeks, which was pretty much everything. It was not the climate or place for cushioned objects. They'd just get mouldy and wouldn't take well to being scrubbed down with industrial cleaners.

Everything was bare and spare and hard. Couple that with almost constant lurching, bouncing and bangs, and enormous amounts of water and slime, and you had a perfect studio for hematoma art with you as the canvas. Each technicolour lump was brushed with colours from hell's sunsets: obsidian, aubergine, vermilion, puce. They were war wounds and medals to display and tell stories about on harbour days. One thing for certain, fishing was not a good vocation for a hemophiliac or people with bird bones. Luckily, I had bones with the density of lead, or I would have been in a lot more pieces than I was before.

I was never more thankful for my hardy European peasant bones than the day I did a flying camel into the stern cockpit feeling particularly jaunty one morning. For once it didn't look like the seventh ring of hell outside—amazing how cheerful I felt when I didn't start the day in mortal terror. Eschewing my usual careful, crab-like clamber, I jumped up and went horizontal. Unfortunately, I stayed horizontal, fell five feet into the cockpit and landed on the huge knobby metal propeller housing.

Before the pain hit, I was aware I couldn't breathe, which helped me stay very still. The entire universe narrowed down to one tiny point—me, crumpled and terrified. I wondered how dearly I would pay for my gymnastics. Out here, help was hours away, not minutes.

I had knocked the wind out of myself and was now left to determine whether or not I had shattered everything from arm-pit to ankle. By that time Paul had come out on deck and, not seeing me, began frantically bellowing my name. I wasn't over-board, but this could be worse. I summoned up a weak mew and raised my free arm. I was lying on my left hip and didn't want to move anything else.

"What the hell did you do now?" he hissed and eased down next to me. His taut, suddenly grey face scared me even more.

No matter what, I had to get out of the cockpit, so we started moving one small part at a time until I was standing again, shaky but okay. Miraculously, my hip bone had missed the housing by a couple of inches, but my rump—what little there was left of it—had not. Several layers of clothes, including the usual four sweaters, had cushioned the rest of me.

That escapade left a monumental bruise worthy of any har-bour day. Slightly horrified by my body inspection, I changed and grabbed the laundry bags. When Bob stopped me for one more congratulations on the smiley, he noticed my poor little paws, winced in sympathy and told me to go see Anne in the office, who would fix me up in no time. She did, God bless her.

Someone was taking care of me. A motherly woman who wasn't just doing her job but had opened her heart to protect and nurture me. Her gentle kindness drew more tears from me than the terrible pain of my hands being soaked in antiseptic solution. As I wept out the fear and pain and loneliness and burbled my apologies, she paused from massaging my hands with antiseptic cream, held me in her arms and rocked me, murmuring over and over, "It's okay, honey. I know, I know. It's so hard. You're such a brave girl." In that hour, I loved her more than anyone on earth and swore I would never forget her.

After she had salved and bandaged each finger she marched her substantial self over to our boat and reamed Paul out for "letting that poor wee girl's hands get so bad" and she "had a good mind to keep her here 'til her hands healed up." She only released me when he promised not to have my hands anywhere near water or slime for at least a week. Because if my hands weren't healed the next time she saw me, she would send me home on the next packer and he would not be welcome in that camp again.

Paul sheepishly agreed and she marched back up to the office to special-order a box of the smallest, heaviest-grade rubber gloves she could find, no charge, to be brought in by float plane the next day with the mail.

Ten days later, Anne stood on the dock, stern-faced, as I held out my healed hands for her inspection.

"That's good honey, that's real good," she said, giving Paul a brief acknowledging nod over my head.

Indian Candy

During the first weeks in Bull Harbour I became enchanted with the notion that I could take a dead animal, hang it in the wind and then eat it. Of course, there was a lot more to it than that, but that was basically it: kill it, dry it, eat it. People all over the world had managed for millennia without refrigeration, for the most part, by preserving food through dehydration. Amazing. Why would just removing moisture keep meat from rotting and killing me?

I was amazed that more fishermen didn't do it with salmon. It wasn't like it would eat into their profits. There was always a belly-cut fish not worth selling or a dead undersized or an illegal fish on a hook. Why throw it overboard? We were out there spending fuel and time anyway; we might as well take advantage of the free groceries. It might have had something to do with the redneck attitude that only poor (read *lousy*) fishermen eat fish. And it wasn't just that they got turned off fish because they had to handle them and were sick of the sight of them. They believed that the only reason you'd eat fish is because you couldn't afford to eat anything else.

So the High Rollers stuffed their boats to the gunwales with steaks and roasts and hams and mountains of junk food. They were the only ones who could afford it and they knew it. It was an ancient form of conspicuous wealth, like potlatches and fat wives. Of course, the irony here was that their wealth was killing them with cholesterol.

The rest of us may have been poor, but we were certainly healthier. We hadn't even caught a cold, for God's sake. Our squeaky-clean diet and intense physical activity must have compensated for indulging in too much beer, coffee and cigarettes. Then there were the jujubes, those cheerful little darlings that called to us from the camp shelves and we could never resist. Funny how such an unassuming thing we took for granted at home became elevated to a guilty pleasure just because it was uncommon out here.

The marine menu pooh-poohed by the High Rollers was coveted by land dwellers, who spent their conspicuous wealth buying the same stuff tarted up in trendy restaurants. But no matter how much they paid, it would never come close to what it tasted like fresh from the chuck. In less than five minutes I could have a little salmon dressed, deboned and in the oven. The oil stove was always going anyway, so why not cook fish while you worked and rolled your guts out?

But where salmon really shone was when it was air-dried. Known as Indian Candy because of its ruby colour and sweet-ish taste, it was one of nature's best fast foods. That's not to say it was quick and easy to make, just to eat. And not that it was always delicious, just when you made it right. And boy did I make it right.

The First Nations people knew what they were doing when they filleted and cut their fish into long strips to dry in the wind.

They knew that direct sun would toughen and seal the outside before the inside had a chance to dry. They knew that wide slabs and chunks wouldn't dry inside either. So do you think the Round-Eyes paid any attention to that? Nope, most of them would just string up a whole flattened-out, deboned salmon from the boom and wonder why it went mouldy. Learn and adapt, gentlemen, learn and adapt.

Occasionally I would be told during harbour days that people thought we were an *Indian boat* because of the racks of salmon hanging from our boom. I was flattered instead of angry. Then they would tell me we couldn't be *Indian* because our boat was too clean. Then I was angry instead of flattered. The same people who made snide remarks about the *predictable* dirtiness and drunkenness of *Natives* seemed to be the ones nursing the worst hangovers on the nastiest-looking boats. Historical resentments and prejudices still simmered on both sides of the racial divide.

In Paul's case, people never could quite figure out his racial pedigree and it took weeks before I was told the reason for the occasional sideways look when we were together. Racial mixing aside, his genetic cocktail of Scottish, English, German, Mohican, African-American and God knew what else had created a specimen that most men wanted to be and most women wanted to have.

I became a culinary bloodhound and sniffed out anyone who had air-dried fish and pumped them for information. Through much trial and error, I devised the perfect technique. I could have won the gastronomic equivalent of a Pulitzer for air-drying salmon. It was so good people told me that I should sell it. I probably could have made more money with it than fishing, that's for sure, but it was so labour intensive I made it only for our use and the occasional free sample, and once as a gift.

Being of the Nordic persuasion, my father was crazy about fish, any kind in any form, but especially pickled and preserved. I got the brilliant idea to surprise him with a Father's Day gift fit for royalty, a box of my very best Indian Candy. I imagined his eyes sparkling with delight at the colour and smell, rhapsodizing over the texture and taste in that contained northern way, murmuring, "What a kid." I also imagined my mother, her Tuscan sensibilities informing him that he would be enjoying my gift in his workshop, as quickly as possible, a value-added scene for my amusement.

Ever the info hound, I discovered the best way to send the salmon was either vacuum-sealed (no chance of doing that up here) or wrapped in many layers of paper towel, then newspaper. Plastic wrap would encourage mould. Besides, it would only be a few days, a week tops, until it arrived in the small BC Interior town of Clinton. It wouldn't smell yet and no one would be the wiser.

Excited as a kid at Christmas, my new pal Anne snuck the salmon on the mail delivery float plane the next day. Loaded with postage, it began its journey from the watery west coast to the arid Interior. Anne and the camp crew were so caught up in the fun of this Father's Day frolic they let me call my dad on their marine telephone to tell him to keep his eyes peeled for the surprise of a lifetime. I had included an eight-page letter and told him he could read about all my adventures while enjoying his gift. He loved the suspense as much as I did. Mum was crying so hard again, I had to share the secret with her on the phone to distract her.

But more suspense than we had bargained for was yet to come, as the salmon went on a little adventure of its own. Everything went swimmingly, until the day it arrived at their small-town post office. Dad had told his pal the postmaster that a very important parcel was on its way and to please let him know the second it arrived. The postmaster was just about to do so when he received a call from his area union rep saying they had begun a wildcat strike as of midnight and all mail currently in his possession was to remain undelivered until the situation was resolved.

Dutifully, the postmaster called Dad to tell him the package had arrived but unfortunately could not be released. My father, who had never done an illegal thing in his life, offered to sneak across the street in the middle of the night and have it slipped through the side window to him. No amount of pleading and cajoling could sway the postmaster: he was a devoted union man and besides, he would be fired if found out.

He told Dad not to worry, the strike would last only a few days. It lasted six weeks. Forty-two days of record-breaking heat, locked windows and doors, no air-conditioning and a smell that increased exponentially. The postmaster had to be there for every single one of those days to guard the mail. Even my gracious father was driven to retort, "Well, I guess you wish now you'd given it to me when it got here. Serves you right." Three feet of Arborite and a labour dispute as turbulent as November gales separated the Druid King from his gift.

On the 43rd day, the postmaster unlocked and opened every window and door, marched across the street and handed my father the salmon-oil-soaked box.

"I could have her charged for sending something like this in the mail."

"You'll have to catch her first," my father said and smiled benignly.

When Dad finally opened it on his back deck, dogs howled, babies cried and birds fell from the sky.

"It wasn't bad at all," he said the next time I called. "I just peeled off a few mouldy ones and the rest were great. Eating them in my workshop seems to work out best. I read your letter and eat the salmon and think of you out there doing all that stuff. It's the best Father's Day present I ever had. You're really something. What a kid."

Even hundreds of miles and a radio telephone between us couldn't conceal my tears. I was living this life for the both of us and he was proud as hell.

Recipe for Sylvia's Superlative Salmon Candy

Catch one small (four- to six-pound) salmon. Humpies are too oily, springs too dry, coho too costly, but sockeye are just right. In a pinch, use what the gods give you.

Before proceeding, remember to tell the fish how beautiful he is and thank him for the gift of his flesh for your well-being and enjoyment. Kill him quickly and compassionately and handle him gently at all times thereafter.

Dress the fish out squeaky, and I mean squeaky, clean. Remove all scales and slime. Do not leave one molecule of blood behind. Transfer to a bleached-clean PLASTIC cutting board. Cut off his head and tail, slit open to both ends and debone, being ultra-careful not to cut through the skin. You should have a flat, rectangular slab of salmon meat backed by skin.

Cover meat with several sheets of paper towel to absorb excess moisture and let rest for an hour in a dry, breezy area away from fumes and diesel exhaust and cinders.

Place another bleached-clean PLASTIC cutting board on top, flip over gently and remove first board to expose the skin. Make sure flesh is flat. Blot skin with paper towel to remove excess moisture, then expose skin side in a dry, breezy, preferably sunny (but not hot) spot for two to three hours to dry and toughen the skin. This is so when you puncture the skin to hang the slab up to dry, the holes won't tear through the skin from its own weight. Bleach-clean the first board.

When the skin is dried and tough, puncture four small holes across the top end of the slab about an inch down from the upper edge. Place the first cutting board back on the skin, flip again and remove the second board and paper towel from the flesh. Bleach-clean the board and put away. Discard paper towel. The flesh should be deep orangey-red and glistening. Take a bleach-cleaned dressing knife and gently score the surface of the flesh in both directions with lines one inch apart to create a checkerboard effect. Then go back and carefully cut the lines deeper, about halfway to the skin. This will allow for air to penetrate the flesh without tearing the skin.

Weave a bleach-cleaned narrow dowel or long bamboo chopstick through the four holes at the top edge. Let rest for one hour to toughen the holes. Try lifting the slab partway up by the chopsticks to see if the holes will hold. If they start to tear, let the slab dry flat for another hour. Keep doing this until you can suspend the slab from the chopstick without the holes tearing.

While the slab is flat, sprinkle the following ingredients lightly and evenly over the cubes and gently rub in, making sure the spice mix gets into the cut-lines. This acts as a marinade for flavour and a curing substance to ensure safe preservation. Rub in this mixture once a day until the meat is completely dried and cured. Use a small amount, as it will accumulate over the days.

fine salt
garlic powder
onion powder
brown sugar
lemon juice (very sparingly)

Do not let the cubes get wet or dirty. Hang outside on the boom; works best in light winds. Hang inside when there is heavy wind, excessive heat or chance of wetness. Direct hot sun dries the outside too quickly and causes the inside to mould. This is a long process: give it approximately a week to ensure safe preservation.

As the skin dries and toughens, it will contract and pull the cubes apart. When this starts to happen, lay the slab down and carefully cut the lines just to the skin, but not through.

As the flesh dries it will shrink and become deep red and shiny. Anything else means mould. When ready, the flesh is chewy and the consistency of jerky, not mushy or tough. It should have only a very subtle fishy flavour.

Not only does cubing the flesh ensure safe and even drying and curing, it also creates convenient bite-sized pieces to pop in your mouth when you're on the run or dirty. It's also a fantastic high-protein lightweight food to carry on hikes. Just remember not to carry it wrapped in plastic, especially when it's warm, as this will create an orgy of bacteria.

The Quick Turnaround

When it comes to split-second timing and perfect choreography, Swan Lake has nothing on The Quick Turnaround. Heaven to some, hell to others, it is the surrealistic state in which an entire fishboat is dumped, cleaned and reloaded in one day—sometimes a few hours. A precision Swiss cuckoo clock at warp speed. It is the state that fishermen dream and pray about because it is usually only necessary when the fish are running hard and your hold is full.

So much about this business is timing. Along with the vagaries of weather, tides and government interventions, there's the endless search for fish and the worry over having enough ice and supplies that you can afford and that will last as long as you need them to. It's not like you can zip over to the corner store if you forget or run out of something, and the results of not having enough can be disastrous. Your boat may run on oil and diesel, but you run on coffee and cigarettes: the fisherfolk's rocket fuel.

The second that crushed ice hits your hold, the 10-day clock starts ticking—that's how much time you have before it melts or your fish flatten or go mushy. Watery ice? Less time.

Forgot to put on ice blankets? Less time. Anchored up in a hot, sheltered bay to wait out the storm? Less time. The longer you stay out, the more layers of fish you lose.

Then there's the running around like a lunatic from one area to another, frantically trying to find fish. The minute you hear of a good score somewhere, it's too late. By the time you get there, closer boats have fished it out or the fish have moved on elsewhere. So you burn up time and fuel and your health for nothing and you limp back to the camp after 10 days to dump your slush and the few rats awash in it. But when all the stars align and all the plates spin on all the sticks just right, you fly into the Quick Turnaround.

We knew it would be a low score again this trip, but the 10-day clock was about to run out of time and Paul had decided to bypass Bull Harbour this time and run down to Port Hardy for more gear and to get our pilot looked at again. It was late June and we hadn't been back to Port Hardy since mid-May. I wondered what it would be like on the verge of the first big opening.

This quick turnaround was going to catapult us over the top of Vancouver Island and down the wild and woolly west coast, where we'd heard they were doing a bit better than this miserable scratching around in the dirty lump that continued day after day at the north end. Coho season was opening in three days, on July 1, and we wanted to hit it hard out of Winter Harbour. Ironically, the very morning we had to run in was brilliantly sunny and calm. I took that as a good omen for our run to Winter Harbour.

We'd been up since 4:30 a.m. to fish the morning bite and had trolled as close into the offshore shelves and reefs as possible, to save fuel and pick up the odd straggler. The nor'wester was picking up pretty good, as it often did in the afternoon. We pointed the bow into the waves and picked up the gear. We'd radioed the camp in Port Hardy and knew they had space and ice for us and an unload time. Paul knew better than to arrive in a fish camp during high season without radioing ahead. He'd seen the boats tied six deep off the finger floats, waiting their lives away.

But we'd be okay; Paul knew the manager and he liked us. Being loyal, bringing in quality fish and helping out with the unload kept us on the company A-list for ice, water, fuel and even pricing at all the camps. They even let us run a tab when things got scratchy. A good reputation could make or break you and was damn near impossible to fix if broken.

While we stashed the gear, we made mental notes on what we had to replace and what we could get by with. I'd set up a system of notebooks for everything we needed and bought, from food to fuel, so I could keep track of our expenses and how much we used. No matter how frugal we were, we barely broke even most of the time.

A shopping list may be more of a wish list, depending on the fish camp, how much you made that trip and how much they have in stock. So you plan your meals out carefully, factor in all the other costs, like fuel, coffee and cigarettes, count your pennies and hope for the best. I'd stood in front of grocery shelves that made Cold War food lines look like Harrods of London.

Most of the time, if the autopilot was working, I dressed the last of the fish and kept watch for other boats while Paul went down to the hold through the deck hatch to pull off the ice blankets and excavate any groceries still tucked away in the ice. He shovelled the top layer of ice onto the hold floor to make sure no over-zealous camp worker accidentally sliced into the first layer of fish. I carefully washed down the wooden deck. No stray guts or slime to slip on or last-minute fish dressing to wait for with our boat. We lifted off the massive hatch cover and laid it on the aft-deck, well out of the way. This was the kind of stuff that kept us on the A-list.

We were getting close to the Nahwitti Bar, which usually required some rodeo-riding and careful navigation, so we hung our Hellys on outdoor hooks by the cabin door and swung into Phase Two. While Paul navigated the channel and checked our electronics, I collected and separated the laundry into three designated green garbage bags.

1. Dirty: underwear, bedding, towels
2. Filthy: socks, bottom-layer shirts and long johns
3. Disgusting: top-layer shirts and pants

I measured powdered laundry detergent into three sandwich bags and counted out quarters for the machines in case I couldn't get to the free ones in time. There was nothing like waiting for your laundry to dry while the skipper frothed and bellowed about getting back out to the grounds.

As we steamed into Hardy harbour, Paul called the camp again to see if we could unload right away or if we'd have to tie up to wait our turn. It was shocking to see so many fishboats in one place at one time. When I read reports of the fleet size it seemed exaggerated: I never saw more than 40 or 50 boats fishing close together, and in off-season, boats were tucked away in hundreds of nooks and crannies along this vast coastline. This was a dog pound of a harbour: boats of every size, shape and condition imaginable. Some like old mongrels limping on three legs, some as sensible and sturdy as black labs and some like primped-up poodles. And everywhere, a circus of noise, action, smells. Bellowing skippers and shrieking seagulls, grinding gears and reeking diesel, airborne ice and flapping fish. After 10 days of isolation it sent me reeling around the deck. If isolation on land was called *bushed* could this be called *waved*? I, the urban groover, felt like a hillbilly down from the hills.

We lucked out and were told to tie up at the unloading dock. By the time we threaded our way to the far end of the camp I had changed into moderately clean clothes, stashed the grocery list and change in my back pocket, put the laundry bags and shower kit on the deck, and dropped the bumpers down on the tie-up side. As Paul nosed into the float and swung the stern in, I grabbed the middle tie-up rope, leaped onto the float and cranked it hard onto a cleat. He cut the engine and threw me the bow and then the stern lines to tie down. We were snug. He threw me the three laundry bags and I stumped my way along the float, up the corrugated ramp and across the dock to the wash house. We hardly spoke a word. I knew what he'd do; he knew what I'd do.

Though I was never seasick, solid land threw me off balance, and I walked like a drunken duck. I ignored the stares and raw yearnings and worn-out offers that came at me like buckshot. This wasn't the first time I'd navigated a man's world. I had already been fending off the advances of a bona fide lech. He made it clear with extravagant offers of less work and more pay that he would not let up until I jumped boats. The fact that I was not only Paul's deckhand but also his girlfriend didn't seem to penetrate his hormone haze. Paul and his pals laughingly referred to him as my *salmon stalker*. I was not amused and took to hiding in the cabin when he was coincidentally in every camp at the same time and would brazenly come onto our deck asking for me. If he was tailing our boat to stay close to me, all he would get out of it was to go broke too. First-aid Anne was no more amused than I, and she let me know she'd had a little chat with him one day in her office that would likely cool his ardour. I never knew the details of that chat, but when we next saw him, he acted like a dog that had had a hose turned on him.

The laundry gods were with me on this turnaround, and as I entered the laundry room, a sturdy old fishwife in gumboots, red mackinaw and flowered kerchief looked me up and down, smiled indulgently and said, "Here ya go dear, you go ahead and take these two free washers, I can wait." For a second, my throat tightened up and I had the urge to curl up in her ample lap and cry, but I just smiled back and thanked her.

Being female in the fishing industry was a lot like travelling in some remote and exotic country. I'd thrill to the sights and sounds, revel in the sheer otherness of it all, but the longer I was gone, the more I secretly yearned for my tribe. And the longer I was gone, the less particular I was. Pretty soon just speaking the same language, or in the case of fishing, being female instantly bonded us. If you were a girl or ever had been, you were my new best friend.

While the first two loads washed I went next door and parboiled myself in the shower. While the first loads were drying and the third load washed, I bought groceries and left them behind the counter. While the third load dried I folded the first two into clean bags, left them on the washer and carried the groceries back to the boat. By the time I returned, the last load was dry and I carried the three bags to the boat.

In the meantime, Paul had helped shovel out the ton of ice in the hold overboard while the fish were hauled out, graded, weighed, tabulated and taken away in bins. He'd hosed and scrubbed the deck, hold, compartment boards, hatch cover and checkers with detergent and collected his fish slip and whatever cash he'd decided to take out of our earnings to pay for fuel and supplies. Sometimes we ran a tab if the trip was poor. There was nothing more demoralizing.

When Paul took our fish book and crew log up to the office to record our catch and workdays for Employment Canada, our take was $634 for 10 days.

We untied from the unloading dock and motored over to the fuel and water dock, where he supervised the fill-up while I put away the dry goods and laundry. Last stop was the ice house, where he rearranged the compartment boards in the hold and directed the stream of fresh ice pouring in through a huge, segmented aluminum pipe. It looked like a dragon's neck and mouth as it reared up from the side of the ice house on a huge boom, then dropped straight down into our hold. The ice travelled up from the ice house on an auger, a massive slowly turning steel screw inside the pipe. Very low-tech but very tough and effective. Not much to go wrong unless someone in the ice house got caught in the auger; then it was all too horrible to even consider.

Once the ice was down, I dropped the perishables to Paul in the hold and he stashed them away. One more tie-up at the regular holding wharf while he showered and shaved and bought and bullshitted and I made up the bunks and planned our meals. With fuel, gear, food and cigs, we'd have just enough left for beer and burgs at the Seagate pub with fisher friends we'd run into at the camp. They'd heard the hotel had just installed a new technology that would show rock videos—the cutting edge of musical entertainment, here at the edge of the world.

Our pilot part had come in on the float plane—another good omen, I figured—and Paul would install it on our way to the west coast of the island the next day, while I steered. All was well with the world and hope ran high as we drank and smoked and laughed and danced the night away. While gyrating to Roy Orbison's "Pretty Woman," a particularly stunning Viking throwback effortlessly lifted me onto his brawny shoulder and I was handed a clutch of red roses bought from a little hippie girl in the bar and anointed Queen of the North to the roars of approving males and my smug, proud boyfriend, whose smile said, "Lust all you want, but she's coming home with me."

We were leaving behind our bad luck and the growing fears that the fish were disappearing—that was all people talked about on the radio and at the camps. Even our pal Gerry, the hottest highliner we knew, couldn't seem to find fish on the north end, even on the Steamer Grounds and Barogh Shoals, 30 miles off-shore. In this game, it was better to laugh than cry, and people dragged tables and chairs over to our growing party, attracted like moths to the bright light of our belief. We vied to outdo each other with more outrageous stories and jokes and damn near choked when one of the old salty dogs cracked up the table by announcing his tab was stretched thinner than a mosquito's foreskin over a 40-gallon drum.

Late that night after we closed down the bar and drank the last of the beer and smoked the last of the cigarettes around Davey's galley table, we heard the story about what had happened to Big John, the halibut fisherman, the previous winter.

In a land of wild excess, of raw survival, Big John was the wildest and most excessive human being anyone had ever seen. His massive, hulking body would fill a doorway, usually to a bar, and the room would fall silent, folks considering the next closest means of escape. He was so vulgar he made even the saltiest dog stammer and blush. Everyone knew he would never go hungry—he had enough congealed food stashed in that mud-brown matted beard to feed on for days. So it wasn't surprising he'd found his way to the West Coast fishing fleet. Lots of misfits hid out here and this wild and dirty life suited him to a tee. Where could he get away with not bathing for days and days? Where else could he wear the same long underwear for months?

The thing about Big John was that he was a working machine. He was virtually indestructible. As long as you had a bunk big enough to hold him and enough food to feed him, he'd work through anything and never complain. In fact, it seemed he hardly noticed the difference between being on land or sea. He was a skipper's dream, if you could stand the smell and lack of conversation.

But it was the harbour time that always got him into trouble. He'd drink 'til he dropped, a long and formidable event. People only had to see him brawling in a bar once. Then it would be time to cruise the docks and look for another job. There was always a skipper looking for a new deckhand and he seemed tame enough.

But even Big John couldn't cheat the sea of its due. One frigid night the past winter, the halibut boat he crewed for went down in a midnight gale north of Cape Scott. No matter what, he was one of our own, and when one was lost it brought the imminence of death a little closer to all of us.

People said he had managed to struggle into a survival suit before the boat broke up but didn't make it to the Zodiac with the other two. He just disappeared in the roaring hell. They said the other two were picked up the next morning by the Coast Guard, much the worse for wear, but still alive thanks to their suits. The search for Big John was hampered by the furious southeast gale but the Coast Guard would keep trying. Everyone knew what the chances of survival after the first 24 hours were for a regular human being, even in a survival suit, but what about someone built like a woolly mammoth?

It was one of the worst storms anyone could remember, raging and hurling itself against the west coast for two days. Not even Big John could have survived, and even if he had, God knows where it would have blown him. Folks figured the Graveyard of the Pacific had cut another notch in its gatepost and wished him good journey to whatever and wherever the Creator had planned for him.

The storyteller's serious face and hushed tones didn't look like good news—we prepared ourselves for a grisly account. "They found him way up near the Charlottes after three days, out there bobbin' around, still alive, barely."

We stared dumbfounded.

Lowering his voice, he leaned in closer over Davey's green Arborite galley table jammed with elbows, bottles and ashtrays. "He pulled through okay, but they say he's not alright in the head. Took him up in the helicopter babblin' away about seein' stuff. Bein' thrown around out there in a blow all by yourself would blow anyone's mind. Poor bastard."

As the frigid halibut season had lurched on, people heard bizarre bits and pieces of what had happened to John out there. Tales of lights and voices and visions and, most surprisingly, of prayers. No one paid much attention to accuracy or reality; it would have ruined a perfectly good story. Everyone knew the creative powers of time, beer and imagination and relished the tellings and retellings in bars and fishboats all along the coast.

Someone ran into the skipper of the doomed halibut boat at the Fisheries dock in Vancouver's False Creek a few months later, and after a little prompting and a couple of beers at the local pub, they got the whole story.

Big John's massive blubbery body and shaggy hair and beard had helped keep him alive, buffered the relentless pounding of waves and wind and kept in his body heat. He wouldn't have starved in three days; his fat supplied the energy he needed to keep his body upright. To save him from dehydration, the deluxe-model survival suit he was wearing had packets of water with attached drinking tubes embedded in the lining of the upper chest. It also had a self-activated blinking light fixed to the top of the close-fitting hood to go along with the brilliant orange colour and the flares stashed in leg pockets.

For two days his powerful body had protected itself, sometimes hurled like a stick, sometimes dragged up and down the roller-coaster waves. By the third night the seas had calmed to a heavy sickening swell, but he had reached the end of his endurance. Feeling there was no hope of rescue, he made the decision to hurry the end and unzip his survival suit. Just before he did, he found himself stumbling through some kind of prayer, an entreaty to something, for help and forgiveness for a life poorly lived.

"Yeah, thanks, I will take that beer to wet my whistle. Wait 'til you get a load of what happened next," the storyteller said and lit another cigarette. Paul pushed a fresh bottle of Labatt Blue across the table to him as we all took a long silent pull on our beers.

As Big John's hand felt for the zipper release, he heard an eerie, unearthly sound, a penetrating hum, and thought he must be dying or having a stroke. It grew louder, and though he had tried to keep his eyes shut to protect them from the corrosive effects of salt water, he opened them to the smothering darkness. Suddenly a pinpoint of light appeared just above the water and slowly grew larger and more nebulous, like a luminous fog.

As he blinked rapidly to clear his vision, the fog seemed to collect into wavering shapes that stretched back into the distance, human shapes that gradually took on bits of detail—a plumed hat, a jewelled sword, a heavy duffel coat, a shell necklace. Every shape and size and feature of human imaginable, some alone, some in clusters.

This endless line of misty figures that hovered just above the waves terrified Big John more than any storm and he screamed, "No. No. Go away. Leave me alone." The gates of hell had opened and they were all evil spirits coming to take him to his just desserts. Closer and closer they came 'til they seemed to cluster around him, drifting and murmuring.

"The damnedest thing about it," the storyteller said, taking a big gulp of his beer and slowly shaking his head, "is that John heard these voices in his head telling him not to be afraid or give up hope cuz it wasn't his time. They told him help would come soon and his life was meant for somethin' else. They told him to keep lookin' up."

John must have fallen asleep, because he woke up to a heavy whump-whump sound through the pre-dawn grey and looked up to see the lights of a huge Coast Guard helicopter coming toward him. The Coast Guard guy said that the pilot was just about to turn to move farther down the coast when he told the crew he'd make one more circle. That's when they saw the tiny blinking light and the glimmer of orange.

It was days before John could talk, weeks before he could tell his story. Though battered and dehydrated, his body recovered amazingly well and quickly. It was his mind they worried about. When he did speak, it was to recount again and again the story of his rescue, how it was the spirits of drowned mariners who had gathered to give him hope, how God had spared him to carry on his work in the world. He spent hours slowly mouthing his way through a King James Bible and attended hospital chapel as soon as he was able.

Apparently one of John's therapists did a little research and it turned out that John's detailed descriptions of his spectral saviours matched historical records of dress, hair and weaponry from the various cultures who had plied those waters in the last 200 years: Spanish and English explorers, Russian trappers, Kwakiutl warriors. How could someone like John, an early high school dropout, have known such detailed information? He was barely literate.

John was eventually released into his mother's care and became deeply involved in an evangelical church group. A few fishermen had visited him and said he was almost unrecognizable. He was lean and quiet and groomed to within an inch of his life. His bellow had been replaced with a whispery monotone.

"But it was his eyes that gave you the willies. Looked right through and past you, like he was always watchin' somethin' far away. Last anyone heard he was a missionary in the middle of Africa, safe from that haunted sea."

With that, we murmured our goodbyes and padded back to our boats to be alone with our mortal thoughts.

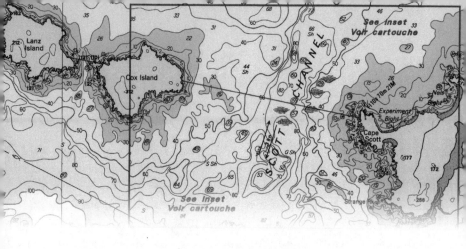

No Atheists at Sea

No matter how many times I scanned the galley or checked the cast-off list or paced the deck, I just couldn't shake that weird feeling of unease that had seeped out of my restless sleep and into the subdued grey dawn. Some undone thing. A little queasiness from the night's revelry. Maybe a lingering eeriness from too many strange stories.

We were already running up Goletas Channel on our long haul over the top and down to Winter Harbour, which Paul figured would take around 10 hours. Normally we would have trolled along the Yankee Spot on the way to save fuel, but the coho opening was in three days and rumours had trickled in that fish were already showing up. Besides, fishing was dead at the top and not worth even throwing in the gear. We'd run down to Sea Otter Cove and troll the rest of the way to Winter Harbour and make it in before dark.

We didn't dare jump the opening like a few fishermen we'd been hearing about, who figured no one at the camp could tell if they brought in a load whose bottom layers were a couple of days older than they should be. Not that it hadn't crossed our minds, considering the difference a couple of $110 cohos would make to us. But was it worth the risk of being boarded by the Coast Guard and tied up for the season?

We were leaving what had become home for the last six weeks, filled with the comfort of familiar voices, faces and landmarks. Bull Harbour's little community was proud of itself and had soon welcomed us into the family. They liked the good lookin' funny guy and his plucky girlfriend who bounced around the floats like Heidi the goat girl.

Past Shushartie Bay, where we'd anchored up with Richard in the first few days a hundred years ago. Past Bull Harbour, where I would have to make amends to the managers for selling our springs in Hardy. Then over the usual lumpy chop of Nahwitti that I'd learned to almost ignore. Then veering west to run a straight course, a mile offshore across the top to save fuel. Past Cape Sutil, where we'd shared dinners with Papa Gerry and relished the care packages of cigs and treats and fishing gear he'd floated over to us in triple green garbage bags. Along the inside edge of the Yankee Spot, where I learned to run gear, dress fish and withstand the endless rain and pounding. Where I'd revelled in the handful of luminous millpond days.

I tried to convince myself that it was just the choppy seas and darkening skies that were making me restless, even though we had often been in worse. Once we passed Christensen Point and veered more southwest, we started losing the protection of the headland and the seas began to kick up odd and jumbled, as if the waves didn't know which way to go.

It had been blowing northwest since the day before, but the weather report said it would switch to southeast by later in the day. Paul seemed confident it wouldn't get bad until later on the west coast and we'd be in Winter Harbour by then.

"Well that doesn't make any sense," I said, reaching to turn on the continuous Coast Guard weather report. "We're travelling the north end that's not protected in a nor'wester, then down the west coast when it's blowing southeast right into us? Listen, it doesn't sound too good. Why don't we wait it out until tomorrow in Fisherman Bay?"

"Ten-to-15 is nothing to run in," Paul said, turning off the radio. "What's the matter with you today?"

"I don't know. I just don't feel right about this." I scanned the rough chop. "One of the fishermen at the bar last night told me that Cape Scott Channel can get pretty tricky between the mainland and some little islands just offshore."

"I was told if you stay in the middle of the channel you miss the rocks and shoals and it'll be okay. We can't waste time screwing around. The coho opening is in three days and we have to get down to Winter Harbour tomorrow to check in at the BC Packers camp and find out what's going on. I'll bet half the fleet is already there. We have to tie a bunch of coho gear and get ready to really start hauling in some fish. Coho is just the start. Wait 'til the pink opening August 1st. They were pulling in 300 a day two years ago and there'll be a hundred boats out there tacking a grid pattern. Think you could handle it?"

"I'd love the opportunity to handle 300 fish a day," I mumbled and went to the open back door, noticing how it was getting a little harder to walk. I felt like a dog sniffing the wind, hackles up. It was getting so dark and nasty out there, it was hard to believe it had been summer solstice a few days ago.

Suddenly, as we rounded the last bit of headland and entered the channel, we were flung into chaos—sharp erratic waves came over the bow and gunwales from everywhere.

"Christ, Paul, what's happening? I've never seen anything

like this before!" I grabbed the dashboard, my heart pounding.

"I don't understand why it's so bad—it's not blowing that hard. Give me the tide book and the chart fast. The fucking loran isn't working so I'll have to use the chart. Shit, I can't let the wheel go. Tell me the fathoms in the middle of the channel."

I frantically searched the chart for the tiny lines and numbers that told us depth. In the middle of the channel, right where we were being thrown around, the depth suddenly jumped up to 15 fathoms.

"Now find out when slack tide is," he said sharply, gripping the wheel and scanning the endless angry water.

"Slack is over, the tide has already turned and the waves are coming in against the tide. Christ Almighty Paul, we have to turn around and get out of here right now."

"Jesus," he hissed. I followed his stare to a dark green wall of water rising straight up, right in front of our bow, higher than I could see above the window.

"Oh my God," I whispered, and felt my heart stumble. A shockwave rushed through my body and I gripped the dashboard to keep from falling. Shutting my eyes and bracing for the wave that would crash over us, I felt myself tip back and opened my eyes to see our boat miraculously climb the impossibly vertical wave, then careen down into the trough. The next crest revealed massive curling waves advancing straight for us as far as I could see, taller and more savage with every pass.

Soon we weren't sliding down into each trough anymore, but teetering on the crests and then falling the 40 feet into the troughs. It was like falling four floors in an elevator, and I groaned like a sick animal; the whole boat shuddered and cried out in pain as it struggled to survive each terrible blow.

Paul glanced at me braced in the corner of the wheelhouse and snapped, "Get below and lie down. You're scaring the shit out of yourself."

"No, I'm not going down there. I'm staying here with you." Everything in me wanted to snarl, *You put us here, you stupid bastard*. Everything in me screamed to fight, to flee—anything but crouch mute and helpless. I struggled to calm my ragged panting. I couldn't bear to lie on my dark bunk as the minutes of my life ticked away. If I was going to die here, I'd die my father's daughter, my eyes open to the world I'd loved so much. I stared mutely at each wave, praying it would not be the one to kill us.

I grieved that I was only 23 and had fought so hard to survive so many things. I thought of my parents and their horrendous loss and was furious that there was nothing I could do to save myself, to fight for my survival. I had never felt mortal terror before, had always danced my way out of life-threatening experiences in nature. Always relied on myself to get myself through. But once again, someone else's shit was colliding with circumstances to put me in harm's way.

I wanted to do something: paddle harder, climb higher, run faster, think my way through this and let my cast-iron constitution get me out of it and heal me later.

Fight like a wildcat, like—like when I was trapped and dragged underwater behind an overturned canoe through rapids and logs and boulders. I'd kicked so hard I was bruised for months from foot to hip. Took years for the numb patches to heal. A calm, still voice inside me had said, *Your boots are jammed under the seat. Pull yourself up by handfuls of clothes and free yourself.* When I did and my head broke the surface, it was to hysterical voices screaming my name.

I screamed only once, when a freak wave hit the side of the cabin so hard the galley cupboards flew open and everything tumbled out. I crawled on the floor to shut the cupboards and turned off the oil stove, then shut and latched the back door to stop the swinging and slamming with each climb and fall. It was impossible to even crawl back to the wheelhouse, so I wedged myself into the corner of the back wall and day bunk. I had saved a pot of spaghetti sauce from that sport and now couldn't save myself.

"We're going to be okay, this is a tough old boat."

The engine shrieked as we climbed higher and steeper.

Please God, don't let it be here.

"Jesus Christ."

Daddy, I'm so sorry.

I crawled on my belly to the wheelhouse, felt the engine grind and howl under me. If we lost power now we'd be killed for sure. The boat leaned horribly to one side on a crest. Dark. Light. Dark. Light. The boat was lifted and flung. I wondered for a moment if I was already dead and didn't know it.

Dragging myself up at the dashboard, I wedged my back into the opposite corner of the wheelhouse, clutching the dashboard rim and the chart rack on the wall beside me.

"Turn around, goddamn it, Paul, turn around," I pleaded. "We can't make it through; you're going to kill us if we keep going."

"We can't turn around, it's too late. The waves are too close together. If I try to turn around we'll be broadsided and sink. We have to keep going."

A sob tore its way up my throat.

"Turn around, Paul, you can do it. You know how to do this. Turn around."

He turned to look at me with eyes burning in a frozen face. "Sylvia, I never meant for this to happen. You're the bravest woman I've ever known. We're gonna be okay. I'm going to get us out of here. Look out the window and start counting the waves out loud as far ahead as you can see. Find two that are a little farther apart and count seven waves. Then the next set until there's one wider than the rest; that's the one we'll turn on."

I felt a surge of energy and we started counting. Louder and louder, over and over.

We saw it coming from a great distance . . . this was our only chance. Neither the boat nor us could hold out much longer. It had to be a perfect turn at the perfect second. If we were broadsided during the turn we would be sunk, and the waves would soon be too close together to fit between them when we fell.

He spun on the crest with a massive shove to the wheel and I heard the prop whine in thin air, then catch the edge of the wave, and we turned just in time before the wave passed. The next wave was straight on our stern, and it lifted us and rushed us forward instead of crashing into our deck and hold. If it had, our cabin would be torn apart. If the hatch cover came off, we would fill up and sink.

We surfed on the massive following sea in huge strange surges that pulled rhythmic groans from the labouring engine. Elated now that the dark mountains no longer loomed over us, I could see land and calmer seas ahead. I squeezed my arms around Paul's waist and held him tight as I smiled up into his face.

"I knew you could do it. We're safe now, aren't we?"

"Yuh, we'll be okay, but I have to pay attention and keep the stern straight on to the waves. Luckily we don't have a flat stern. It's harder for the waves to lift and move past. Uh, I wouldn't look out the back window yet; it can be a bit scary with a big following sea."

Of course I ignored him and looked—and then reeled back,

stunned by the mountain that loomed just behind our stern. My heart raced again and I fled to the wheelhouse. Panted and listened to the prop whine as the boat struggled to lift with every surge and I willed the land closer. We would run into the closest sheltered bay and anchor there until the next day, when we would run the channel again at high slack tide and closer to the shore in deeper water.

Slowly the waves shortened and broadened as we cleared the channel and turned to run deep into Experiment Bight's sheltered waters. We never spoke of that *perfect storm* of circumstances that had nearly taken us. Not then, not ever. We went about our business as if nothing had happened and Paul's brisk matter-of-factness and the way his eyes slid away from my face made that clear. When he said he was a little tired and would take a nap on the day bunk, I said I would *tidy up* a bit and maybe catch up on some reading.

I was in an agony of aftermath with no one to help me work through it. No one to help me dump out the jumbled box of thoughts and feelings and images to inspect them, to hold each to the light before wrapping and rearranging them according to their connections. Even my journal was little comfort. I quickly recorded just a few truncated sentences so I wouldn't have to read the enormity of it later and then quietly made it all go away.

Pretty much everyone did that out here—downplayed or mocked or bragged the terrors and revelled in the good—it was the only way to survive where life was in the balance every moment. Where we lived on the knife edge of extremes. For many, it was a drug and a lover they couldn't quit; to do so would be to live in the careful, grey world of moderation.

I had swum to the canoe that eventually got me to shore. I had clung to the gunwales while my friends fought through the rapids, my heart singing with joy at the world's beauty, while I was pulled numb and blue through the spring runoff waters for nearly an hour. My burning spirit and my father's wool sweater that my mother had lovingly knit him had kept me from slipping away from this world at 20 years old, had me running down the beach an hour later to find the others while my rescuers collapsed on the shore.

Now I found myself out on a fishboat deck, slowly turning in a circle, drawing in the beloved breath of the sea, filling my lungs, my belly, my brain, with the brightening light and lifting skies, the coquettish whitecaps, the perfect crescent moon of beach. Facing the churning channel, I slowly pulled off my baggy old pullover, then the long-sleeved T-shirt damp with sweat and fear, and let them dangle then fall to the deck; unhooked my bra and dropped it to the pile; unzipped my faded Levis and let them and my white cotton underpants fall to my feet; closed my eyes and tilted back my head and let the last of the westerly wind blow over and through me and pull the fear and rage from me, to wait in the place of a thousand sorrows. I reached and stretched high on my toes, the air electric with life.

When I tiptoed past the day bunk to the fo'c'sle, clothes under my arm, Paul stirred in his sleep. I paused to watch his weary face and was aware for the first time of the gulf of years between us, his dark good looks and electric sexiness receding in the hardened eyes and deeply etched lines. I longed to lie with him, to caress him to wakefulness, but I wouldn't risk another rejection that I would never understand. Instead, I dressed in clothes fresh from the previous day's laundry and stowed my sad little bundle deep in the corner of the storage bin beside my bunk, under the extra canned goods and gear. I knew I would never wear them again.

By the time I finished tidying up, the sun was coming out and Paul sleepily offered to go to shore with me to look for glass balls. Used as floats on Japanese nets, they were now quite rare, travelling thousands of miles over the Pacific to west coast beaches. Everything was light and bright with chatter about glass balls and beaches as we ate a quick salmon sandwich and prepared for our favourite event: exploring somewhere new.

Paul rowed us into shore on a slack wind and I was thankful for the smooth ride into the postcard beach. We dragged the skiff up the beach and couldn't find anything to anchor the bow rope, the glistening crescent was swept so clean and white. Grass-covered bluffs on either side of a sandy spit filled with twisted trees and sand dunes led like a corridor to the stunningly beautiful beach of Guise Bay that opened its long graceful arms to the west coast. Speechless, we stood on the bluff and absorbed the almost unearthly beauty of sand and sea and dense, deep forest, luminous in the warm southeast breeze.

As we descended the spit into the low dunes leading to the beach, I noticed tall crooked slats of weathered wood marking an irregular arc across the dunes and almost tripped over the corner of something half-buried. Kneeling down, I brushed away the sand to reveal a small square metal plaque that told us this was the site of a Danish settlement in the late 1800s. The slats were remnants of a wooden fence windbreak built to halt the drifting sand.

Exploring the dense woods that rimmed the beach, we found tumbledown old cabins, some still used as shelters by campers. Lovely wildflowers, maybe the descendants of gardens, grew everywhere: cobalt lupines, lavender columbines, bright-faced daisies. We followed another small wood sign on to the Hanson Lagoon trail, some of it on a raised wooden boardwalk that led for 10 miles through the forest to Hanson's Lagoon, farther down the coast where the settlers lived and farmed as well. We walked a couple of miles on the trail, mostly in silent single file, relieved to be away from the confines of boat life and enjoying the free swinging movement of our bodies. I felt drawn to know more about the settlers, what had brought them to this incredibly wild and remote place and what drove them away.

Since there wasn't another human in sight and it had been blowing for two days, we had a chance of finding a glass ball amid the satiny bleached logs that ringed the fine, hard-packed sand. Excited as a kid on an Easter egg hunt, I found five little beauties the size of large oranges, tinted in delicate shades of aquamarine and fern green. They fit in the front-zipped pocket of my anorak.

By the time we wandered back to our skiff in the opposite bay, the breakers were three feet high and curling into the beach from the powerful incoming tide. We studiously timed the skiff shove-off and counted the waves for the second time that day. Careful to not get our sneakers wet in the surf, we rejected wave after wave, until we were certain we had our break, pushed hard and leapt in with precision technique, ready to start rowing like mad. The wave had other ideas, and an instant later we were hit by surf that sent me flying off the bow and Paul off the stern into the chuck. We staggered back to shore laughing our guts out and *very* refreshed by the icy sea water. Since we were already soaked to the skin we just waded past the surf, clambered aboard the skiff and rowed to the boat. Luckily, the glass balls were tied around my waist in my anorak and made it through the adventure.

Thankful for the afternoon sun, we stripped on deck and hung our clothes on the boom and fell into each other's arms, still laughing until our lips met in a sudden flurry of kisses that flung us to the deck.

At sunset, as I sat on the hatch cover reading *The Three Ways of Asian Wisdom,* our old friend the humpback rolled past us on his way to dinner. I thought of the Danish settlers and their moss-covered dreams, Buddhism's *eternal now*, of Sisiutl rising from the waters to test our courage and authenticity, of the song that says *all we are is dust in the wind*. And as the Milky Way blazed its way across the night, I knew for certain one thing: there were no atheists at sea.

Winter Harbour

As much as a 20-ton fishboat can tiptoe, that's what we did, in the pre-dawn run to Winter Harbour. The restless greys of wind, waves and cloud were a perfect backdrop to the inside of our cabin and my psyche. The taste of death still sharp on our tongues, we went about the business of thwarting the Grim Reaper with a carefully calculated approach to navigating Scott Channel, working out the tides, depths and winds to tip the odds more in our favour. Pale and silent, we stood in the wheelhouse, hyper-alert and vigilant, as the outgoing low tide swept us through the channel and revealed the obstacle course of rocks we had to skim by as we hugged the close shore.

I may have been the picture of stoic calm, but I was in pitched battle with every part of me that fought not to be in this place again. I had to beat the flashes and fears back, or I would never be able to go on. Beat them back as I had done during that fateful canoe trip through the Fraser Canyon. Three hours after I had been trapped under the canoe, I had to get back in it, cross the river to find safety for the night and then paddle another two days down the river to get home. I had seen others bested by the terrors and never venture out on the water again.

The gift of our glorious afternoon in Guise Bay had been replaced by a sinister little Jack-in-the-Box as we rounded the point and met the west coast waves full on. These weren't the horrifying mountains of yesterday, but a dirty slop that bucked and rolled us as we ground our way to Winter Harbour. Every once in a while a thought would dart in to let me know I really should consider being afraid, to which I would inwardly snort and remind myself that we had already experienced the worst and still lived to tell the tale, and this? This was just annoying. We had savvied up quick about Cape Scott, and after the heart-pounding approach the previous afternoon we knew the nature of this beast and how to appease it.

I knew Paul wasn't being reckless this time; we wouldn't be running and fishing in bad conditions if we weren't so desperate. In spite of all the uncertainties and terrors, I loved this life and was smitten by its power to strip us humans of our uppityness and constantly remind us of our place: a grain of sand, a drop of water in an endless sea.

To distract ourselves from the relentless pounding, we invented a music game we called Stump the Lump. We were both music lovers, and since the boat stereo had been stolen from Paul's VW Jetta earlier that spring along with the Blaupunkt car stereo, and since the insurance wouldn't cover the boat stereo and we didn't have the money to replace it before we left, we had learned to live without it. The Jetta was a reminder of how lucrative fishing had been until just two years ago—as were travel, art school, good restaurants, designer clothes and other fineries.

As I gripped the dashboard to keep upright, I would sing a melody. Paul had to guess the song title and artist, and if correct, he would then play a melody on his harmonica while I steered and guessed. This amused us for several hours until we started to get worn out by the rough ride, which worsened the closer we got to the point at the northern opening to Quatsino Sound that would eventually lead to Winter Harbour.

Our choice was either to ride farther south into the open roiling waters past the rocks and islets of the sound and then double back to run to the inlet that wound its way inland to harbour, or cut the trip shorter and risk the narrow channel of huge crashing waves and rocks between the point and Kains Island lighthouse and run straight into the inlet. Longer and awful, or shorter and hellish.

After my eyes popped out of my sockets at the sight of the channel, Paul asked me if I was scared. I decided on "a little" considering the nightmare we'd been through just 24 hours ago and how worn out we were from the trip down. I was pissed that he was even considering the channel option, as he didn't know it very well. He seemed almost relieved that one of us had admitted to being afraid and rounded the islands to surf our way to the back of the Sound and through the five miles of twisting, lowland inlets freckled with humpbacked islands covered to the glassy water's edge by dense evergreens and salal shrubs. I never got over the dramatic shift from chaos to calm, freezing to furnace, once we were out of the wind and into sheltered waters. One minute I was shivering in layers of wool and rubber, and the next, tearing my clothes off as the mercury shot up. Today was a miracle of peaceful warmth.

Until we rounded a corner and the clamour of two fish camps and hundreds of boats came at us across the water like a gale. Paul was right. Half the fleet must have been jammed into the bay of this miniscule hamlet, a haven for ships since the 1800s. Winter Harbour had the only fish camps for almost another hundred miles down the west coast, offering fishermen the options of selling to BC Packers, the Fisherman's Co-op or the occasional cash buyer who hung around just outside the harbour and sold for higher prices but supplied no fuel or ice. In those cases, fishermen could buy ice from the camps, if it was available; preference was always given to fishermen who sold to the camps too. Cash buyers were a good option for day catches, or if you were leaving the grounds for a while, but you never wanted to push your loyalty luck with BC Packers.

With a population of 20, Winter Harbour was connected by a network of publicly accessible logging roads that serviced the northern end of Vancouver Island, linking frontier communities like Coal Harbour, Port Alice and Holberg, which traditionally relied on logging and fishing but were already beginning the shift to eco-tourism and sport fishing. An ancient network of trails by First Nations, then the Scandinavian settlers, criss-crossed the region, and recovery was already underway to reopen many of them.

As in many coastal towns and villages I'd seen, the homes and sheds were jumbled close together along the waterfront, many on stilts, and were joined by a boardwalk that ran the length of the village over the mud flats and water. As we motored toward the BC Packers camp to tie up and check in for ice, fuel and water, I knew that boardwalk would be my sanity in the weeks to come.

I was struck by the realization that these were the round piney hills my father had logged 25 years earlier out of Holberg, the largest floating lumber camp in the world, and cringed to think he had been part of the destruction of the old-growth forests that had covered most of northern Vancouver Island.

I was indeed my father's daughter, here participating in the destruction of the salmon industry. I shook away the irony and prepared to drop the bumpers and tie up to the fourth troller out from the finger float.

The whole bay was buzzing with anticipation of the opening in two days that people desperately hoped would compensate for the miserable spring and sockeye season. Weather reports predicted good weather for July 1 and we were swept up in a flurry of preparations for a 10-day trip in our new neighbourhood. While Paul tied miles of red gear I ran back and forth between the laundry room and our cranked-up stove, preparing pots of stew, chili and spaghetti sauce and putting them down in the ice in plastic containers so I could focus on pulling gear and dressing fish on the grounds.

As much as I loved the familyness of Bull Harbour, I loved the energy of Winter Harbour and had even spotted a few girls my age—we'd smiled and waved happily. During a laundry jaunt I met one of the girls I'd seen on a big steel troller, and within minutes Cheryl and I became best friends. As we sat on our washers, then the dryers, we poured out our life stories, and we soon toured each other's boats, met each other's skippers and planned a communal dinner for that night with four other boats.

She and Craig were just pals, and as much as she loved fishing and was a fantastic deckhand, the rough west coast waters were cooking up a level of seasick she'd never experienced, and she refused to give in to it. There was a genuine camaraderie and respect between them, and Craig shared with us that night that a top-notch female deckhand was worth more than any transgression, no matter how lonely or hormone-driven he might be. He had a girlfriend at home and was out there to make money, not mess around.

The same could not be said for all the fishermen with female deckhands, especially Dirty Ol' Frank, who had a reputation as long as the fishing rod he liked to brag about and had offered to every girl who trod his deck. Some ran screaming or crying or angry from the old codger, but at age 74 he had met his match.

One of the four boats invited to dinner was Frank's, and though he deferred to the young folks, his deckhand, the buxom, blond Danni, happily accepted. We had met briefly at the beginning of the season in Port Hardy, and when Paul had recovered from gawking, he told me that she was in for it with the old bugger. Two months later she was still with him, more strapping than ever, and as soon as was decent, Cheryl and I took her out to the stern of Craig's boat.

"So, Danni, we were wondering how things are going," I said, taking a sip of my beer and reaching up to light her cigarette. "Everything okay?"

"Us girls have to stick together," Cheryl said, opening Danni a beer. "We just want to make sure Frank isn't giving you a hard time . . . you know. You can tell us."

"I'm just fine, don't worry," Danni said and flashed her Colgate smile. "For the first few weeks he was good as gold, talking about how he was getting older and that I was totally safe with him and he thought of me as a daughter. That part was fine, but what was really starting to bug me was that we hardly ever went fishing. One excuse after another and I needed money for school and I just wanted to get the hell on with it and not be on a holiday."

"Well, people have been rolling their guts out for the last two months for nothing, so you haven't been missing anything," I said.

"So did he try anything?" Cheryl said, frowning.

"One morning, after staying tied up for three days, Frank came up from the fo'c'sle completely dressed, including gumboots, but minus his pants and gaunch and says, 'How about you come join me down in my bunk?'"

"Oh my God, naked?" I snickered.

"Yup, with his little-old-man dick hanging down below his flannel shirt."

"What did you do?" Cheryl asked.

"I said, 'Frank, get back down there and put your pants on right now or I'll beat the shit out of you,' and he just stands there with his mouth open, staring, then shuffles downstairs and comes back up, pants on, and asks me what I'd like for breakfast. I said, 'I'd like to catch some fucking fish or I'm off this boat.' So he says, 'We'll go out after breakfast,' and we've been out there ever since."

Cheryl and I burst out laughing and damn near choked on our beer. We kept laughing harder and harder 'til the three of us were hanging off each other and staggering around the deck. It must have been an inspiring sight, because several older fishermen watched, enraptured, from their decks and the float.

Danni could have broken him in half over her knee. After the incident he was as meek as a lamb as she worked him relentlessly and wouldn't let him take harbour days unless the weather was life threatening. He followed her with puppy-love eyes and treated her like a queen, gave her an extra bonus after each trip and upped her share to 15 percent. And when eyebrows were raised at that well-known signal, he tut-tutted and said there was none of that business and she had earned it fair and square and then some— that she ran a tight ship and had made him into an honest man.

His cabin was spotless, she wouldn't allow drinking on board, cooked only healthy food and made him cut way down on his smoking. He even cleaned up his language and no longer made lewd comments about every female within eyeshot—when he had, she'd given him one of her thunderbolt looks and a lecture on respect and equality. She had overheard him once say that if only he had met a woman like that when he was younger, he would have walked the straight and narrow and been a major highliner.

After we collected ourselves enough to join the others, we shared the best we had to create a royal feast of fish and crab and mussels fresh from the sea, wine and special coffees—every lovely little treat we had secreted away on our boats. We toasted life and love and loads of coho and laughed and talked and sang the night away, weaving back to our boats with the birds. We had a whole day to recover and anchored in a quiet clutch behind the last island before The Gut, ready to fling ourselves into the morning.

Calm out there may have been like rough in Bull Harbour, but we were catching fish! Hallelujah, we were catching fish: 30 or 40 coho a day and a couple of springs, which made the rodeo-ride through The Gut every morning worth it. Hell, up at the Yankee Spot we had been banging around just about as bad and going broke for the privilege of it. I got used to my feet leaving the ground with every wave just outside the channel, but by the time we were 10 miles offshore, trolling up to Sea Otter Cove and back, it was usually sunnier and calmer. For a couple of days, just long, slow swells came down from the north, which meant they must have had a mother of a storm up there the day before.

We had been hitting it hard for nine days: running in every night to anchor either in Sea Otter or behind the channel island in Quatsino, usually around 10 p.m., doing a cleanup before falling into bed, then up at 4:30 a.m. for a morning bite. We were almost relieved when the weather started to really kick up and the fishing slowed down. We ran into Winter Harbour to sell our load and wait out the string of southeast storms they said was coming.

I had dressed every fish except the springs for most of the trip. My time was down to 45 seconds a fish—I was training myself for the hump opening coming up August 1, just three weeks away. We might pull in a couple of hundred fish a day; what the little humps lost in value, at just a couple of bucks apiece, they made up for in volume. My hands were small and I was fast as hell, and we'd already decided that when humps opened, Paul would pull and ice and I would dress and drop.

Waiting all day to unload would normally be an agony of frustration when the fish were running and the weather was good, but today for once the timing was perfect: it was blowing like hell on the outside and we needed a harbour day anyhow. Our tally had come in at just under $3,000, the best yet, but it would be just enough to cover the boat mortgage back payments (which couldn't be extended one more month), get the unreliable pilot fixed in Port Hardy so I could pull gear instead of steer, and pay for fuel and groceries at the outrageously inflated camp prices. How many times would we have to tell ourselves that next trip we would start getting ahead?

Over coffee and cigs with Craig and Cheryl at Shirley's Diner, we bitched about our pilot and how we would get it to Port Hardy, and in a flash Craig had the solution: he had to drop off Cheryl in Port Hardy and pick up his new deckhand, so he would take his boat to Coal Harbour, where he had left his truck, then drive all of us to Port Hardy. It was only 30 miles east and back again, an overnight stay on his boat and back the next day. We knew Craig well enough to know we were in for a wild and crazy couple of days. We were not disappointed.

Led Zeppelin blasting, we emerged from Winter Harbour's inlet to a full-on southeast gale blowing into the back of Quatsino Sound that we rocked and rolled and smoked our way across. Luckily, the pot in those days didn't paralyze you with paranoia, and it eased the crossing into Quatsino Inlet—along with the go-go dancing on the deck to Steppenwolf's "Born To Be Wild." We were invincible as wave after wave came over the bow, and we sang harmony to the storm's roar, our blood howling in our veins. Winding through the inlet, we finally shot through the narrows and across to Coal Harbour as slack tide shifted and the whirlpools began to spin again, just like one of those old Jason and the Argonauts movies where gods and demons test them relentlessly.

We piled all four of us into the front seat of Craig's truck and drove the 30-mile neck of land between the west and east coasts of Vancouver Island and went to raise hell in Hardy. We ran into everyone we knew in the world, and drank too much, ate too much, danced too much and laughed too much for any mortal being. But since we were immortal, the rules of this world didn't apply to us, and after a final goodbye to the fantastic band from Seattle that we'd closed down every bar in town with, we wove our way back to Coal Harbour. After a brief nap, gallons of orange juice and a mountain of Aspirins, we motored back to Winter Harbour and our wee bunks, subdued and deeply satisfied.

And as we sat together after dinner on our boat with Craig

and his new deckie, Alex, a brilliant flash of emerald green and ruby red streaked through our open window and fluttered its tiny humming self against the front window. I reached my cupped hands to the creature, and as it touched my palms, it suddenly lay still, and I was transfixed with the miracle of its exquisiteness. Moving slowly through the hush I stepped onto our deck and lifted my hands as the bird shot upward and spun itself toward the setting sun.

The Great Grey Beast

When it is only 4:30 in the morning, and the wind keens and clangs through your rigging, it is a bad sign. When you are still tied to a wharf in a sheltered harbour, and your boat shifts and strains around you, it is a very bad sign.

My damp, chilly shelf of a bed was a thousand times preferable; bankruptcy, starvation, even homicide, were preferable to what I knew waited for us just around the corner—a howling Grey Beast with a taste for wood and bones raging down the inlet, flinging itself against the sheltering wooded walls of that tiny harbour. And who would be foolish enough to pit themselves against this monster? Fisherfolk . . . desperate with worry and exhaustion.

The gods and government had conspired to set a deadly stage: no fish, terrible weather, closures, strikes, cutbacks, rocketing interest rates and falling fish prices. People took bigger and bigger risks, hoping for the miracle that would pay their mortgage and feed their kids. Many would drown in debt, in liquor, in despair. Some would be eaten alive by the Great Grey Beast that waited for us all.

Paul said we couldn't afford to take another harbour day—we were flat broke, "not a goddamned nickel left," even in the change jar. Ours was not the only tab discreetly kept in the camp accounts, but it might have been the longest. We were going out and that was final. So I was just to shut up and go below if I couldn't stand it. But of course I had to stand it; what else could I do but pray and go numb?

I was ashen before we even ran The Gut—a churning, rock-infested channel that spits you out into the inlet or open ocean, depending on which way you are going. It must be what the gates of hell look like. Everything was black and bilious, and I couldn't tell where the sky ended and the water began. I couldn't imagine it could get worse until the erratic sharp waves crested white and started crashing over our bow. First thing you learn about the west coast: it can always get worse.

I staggered up the fo'c'sle stairs into the wheelhouse, lurching from one handhold to the next. Nobody should have to be thrown around like that before the sun comes up.

"What the hell are you doing up here?" Paul growled.

"I wanna see my name on the wave that's gonna kill me," I snarled back.

We couldn't use stabilizers because they'd tear off on the rocks—they were that close—so it was like riding a 20,000-pound Brahma bull. I braced in the wheelhouse, knees bent, feet apart, hands clutching the thick wooden dashboard rim, and still my feet left the floor with each crashing wave.

"Don't you think it's a little odd that it's only 7:00 a.m. and people are already beating their way back in?" I said. "Is that telling you something?"

"We'll go see how it is," he said. "There's lots of people behind us."

Lots was an exaggeration, but there were a few boats bouncing around, waiting their turn to shoot through. It was so narrow there, only one boat could go through at a time—not a problem unless people were running in for their lives, which I suspected would happen fairly soon. Nothing I said, no amount of reason or sanity, could change his mind.

"You have no right to put my life at risk like this. This is insane. The farther out we go, the worse it is. Listen to what they're saying." I turned up the volume on the radio. There were some attempts at false bravado, but the rest were picking up their gear or just plain turning around and running back in.

"I said get down below if you can't take it," Paul said, turning off the radio.

"Take what? Drowning? Being smashed to bits? What the hell is the matter with you? Even if we get back in one piece, we'll probably wreck our gear. The wind will just throw stuff all over the place."

Something black and hard slid down behind his eyes. "I said we're going to go out and try it. We can't afford another day off. You run the wheel and I'll set the gear. Just watch out for other boats."

Cutting the engine to trolling speed, he waited for me to take the wheel and then stomped out of the cabin.

I knew he hadn't told me to steer to give me something to do. It was just too rough to use the autopilot; I would have to manually keep us on tack. I felt like Captain Ahab, lashed to the huge wooden wheel, wrestling with the sea. I watched the few other boats flail and plunge, awash with breaking waves, and knew how horrific we must look to them.

I stretched up to turn on the radio and heard a string of subdued, strained voices advising and agreeing to go in. Fisherfolk are very reluctant to see anyone stay out in such dangerous conditions and often risk their own boats and lives to rescue others.

"We take care of our own," they say. "Who else is going to?"

The BC government, in its infinite fiscal wisdom, had cut the Coast Guard fleet down to three boats for thousands of miles of convoluted coastline. And so the Graveyard of the Pacific continued to earn its name.

The marine forecast suddenly upgraded to gale-force winds and posted a warning to all north and west coast traffic. Again, the forecast had been inaccurate and late. Many people blamed it on the lighthouses going automated. The running joke in the fleet was which lighthouse would break down next and for how long. No more friendly face behind that flashing light, just clicks and whirs.

Wrestling the lurching wheel, I was awash in rage and fear and pity for all us poor souls who were risking everything for nothing. I wondered how much more of this I could stand. I wondered how many more seasons the entire industry, this whole way of life, could stand. Terrible storm clouds were gathering there too: secret meetings, deals and documents, talk of fish farms and Native land claims, conspiracy theories to rival Watergate.

"The glory days are over. Get out while you can," some people said.

"It's just a couple of bad years. Get a bigger boat," others said.

I watched someone in a nearby boat struggle to bring in his gear, lines and hooks flying and tangling around his head. Everything seemed airborne as the wind and water screamed and shoved at us. Suddenly the back door burst open.

"Turn us wide to starboard and start running in at half-speed. I'll keep pulling in the gear," Paul bellowed.

"Thank God," I whispered, but my relief was tempered with a terrible foreboding. You never pull gear while running—you'd probably lose and snarl most of it—unless you are in even more danger if you take your time.

I forced myself to narrow my focus to the treacherous channel several miles away. I couldn't think of what it would be like when we got there—three hours worse than when we went out? I forced myself to breathe slowly, to keep my muscles limber and my brain alert. I remembered a line from Frank Herbert's sci-fi novel *Dune*: "Fear is the mind-killer."

"Push it slowly to three-quarter speed," Paul thundered from the cockpit.

That meant he was either almost done or about to cut all the gear off, but it definitely meant we were in serious trouble. It was so rough I couldn't steer from the seat and instead had to stand, knees deeply flexed to withstand the slamming. I *willed* the channel closer and told myself the lovely lie: I can see trees. I'll be OKAY. Just as I started to make out individual trunks, Paul crashed through the door, gumboots and rain gear streaming, grabbed the wheel and shoved the throttle full open. "Get yourself somewhere safe, it's gonna be a rough ride in." No shit.

I wedged myself into a corner of the wheelhouse, bent my knees and hung on for dear life. I played the Getting Closer game: hold your eyes shut for as long as you can and open them to see how much closer you are to land.

"Stop fucking torturing yourself. Get below," he snapped.

I was mute as I took in his stony face and twitching jaw muscles. I wondered what would happen when the 20 boats I could see all got to the channel at the same time.

The Grey Beast knew the channel mouth was its last chance. I imagined it hoped we would save it some work by running into each other, and it was furious when we did not. It shrieked and lunged and snapped as one by one we were hurled into The Gut.

Just as we cleared the channel, we saw a familiar boat approaching. He couldn't have been considering going out. As soon as we moved into calmer water, we radioed him.

"Fishing's no good here and I just dropped off my deckhand in Winter Harbour. He had to go home, so I thought I'd run 'round to Bull Harbour," Dan said in his usual Perry Como drawl.

We were flummoxed. Calm, sensible Dan was going to run alone, in a gale, through the worst waters on the coast. I mouthed, "Has he gone insane?" Most of us tried to talk some sense into him. He finally agreed to leave his radio and mouse on and periodically let us know he was still okay.

Utterly exhausted, we anchored behind a small island halfway down the inlet to rest and wait to see what the weather would do. It was another five miles through the twisting inlet to Winter Harbour, and if the weather settled down by the following day, we would go out again, saving us the extra 10 miles of fuel costs. We also knew we could keep Dan in range much longer from here.

For the moment we were safe, but Dan was not. I lay on my bunk, sweating and shaking, heart racing with the release of terror and rage. I braced against my inner storm as I listened to Dan fighting his.

I'd always loved radio plays; one Vancouver station still aired them late Sunday nights. I'd turn out the lights and burrow deep in my blankets, making movies in my head. But this was real life; I was not safe in my bed at home and I did not want to see the movie my head was making.

Hour after hour we heard the winds scream louder, the waves hit harder. We heard his voice whittling away. We heard crashes and clatters and held our breath 'til he calmly reported which piece of rigging had just come down. I wept and prayed for him, for all of us, for the salvation of this magnificent and terrible way of life, for the preservation of the Wild West and the demise of its domestication.

The next terrible crash threw us from our bunks and I sank to my knees, sobbing into my hands. Faintly we heard him, his voice fading in and out, eerily calm.

"If you can still hear me, this is probably my last message. My mast has come down and my aerial is going under. I'm in my survival suit and I've tied an orange float around my waist so they can find my body easier. When they find me, tell them to look for the letter in a plastic bag inside my shirt. It's for my wife and kids. Tell them I'm sorry. Tell them I love . . ."

Then nothing, the hissing of dead air, then frantic voices calling, "Dan! Dan!" "Can you hear me?" "Don't give up." Someone called a mayday into the Coast Guard. Everyone knew it was pointless.

I cried so hard I turned inside out.

And it was only noon.

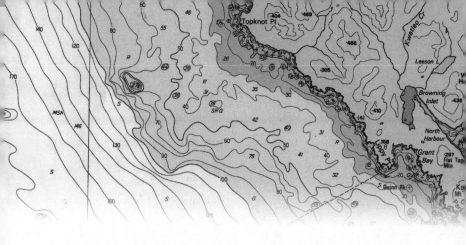

High-Pressure Fronts

A string of sou'easters pushed us steadily up the west coast of Vancouver Island from the roaring seas of Estevan south of Winter Harbour as we chased the last stragglers of the coho run all the way back to Cape Scott and around the corner. Our ears pricked, we sifted through the obtuse messages coming over the radio telephone for clues to where the next hot spot would be. Trouble was, by the time we deciphered the coded comments between group members and ran like stink to get there, the fish had usually moved on.

But when we heard Papa Gerry's lilt suggest we meet him "for dinner in the usual place," we threw it in the bucket at Sea Otter Cove and ran like hell to the Yankee Spot off Fisherman Bay and dropped the gear. The tip couldn't have come at a better time: we had just deep-sixed another shipment of gear to Davy Jones's locker on some pinnacle just outside the cove that seemed to magically change location every damn time, as if it was crouched under the land shelf and waited for us to wallow by so it could leap up and grab a mouthful of gear. A very expensive meal at $300–400 a serving.

To top things off, as Paul raised a trolling pole to capture a pig float that had come loose when our steel gear lines snapped, our second radio aerial broke off and fuelled a total shitstorm of yelling and cursing, much of it aimed at me. Something snapped inside me.

I roared right back at him. "Stop taking your shit out on me. I have my own shit and don't take it out on *you*. I'm just as worried sick about not making money and I'm the one who has to wait another year to go back to school and somehow find the money to pay the bloody divorce lawyer. I don't even have a goddamned place to live since that bastard I married secretly moved back into the house and threw out my renter. And he has the goddamned nerve to be vindictive to me? He leaves me for another woman after my car accident then comes whining for me to take him back a year later? Then gets pissed off when I don't? Are you kidding me? And my parents are freaking out because I haven't been fooling them with my chirpy little collect calls. And I've kept this all to myself because I didn't want to burden you with it, you asshole. But that doesn't stop *you*, does it?"

Stunned and silent, he stepped back as I wheeled away from him and into the cabin. I had never laid into him before. Either I turned myself inside out being princess cheerful or retreated into frenetic activity or the pages of a book or, if all else failed, cried in my bunk, my face buried in the pillow. But I had woken in the cold, wet dawn of that morning with a severe case of existential angst. I was sick of cleaning and tying gear, of trying to catch up on my million-hour sleep deprivation, of manifesting meals out of thin air. I was sick of wondering when that evil pilot part would arrive in Port Hardy. I was sick of the same old ridiculous stories, of drinking coffee and smoking cigarettes. I was sick of worrying and most of all, I was sick of being me. I just wanted to climb out of my skin and trade it for someone else's. I had never felt like that before.

Flinging the last "don't you ever," I slammed the cabin door behind me and started rearranging the cook pots at maximum volume. A few minutes later, Paul quietly knocked on the door, which threw me a bit. When I opened it, he was bent over with his bum in the doorway. I couldn't help but giggle, and when he turned to look over his shoulder with a smug smile and then turned away as if he was perfectly safe in his gesture, I took a couple of deep breaths and kicked him so hard that he flew forward and barely caught himself before falling flat.

He turned to me in shocked surprise and gingerly rubbed his bum. "Jesus, I didn't think you'd really do it. I won't be turning my back on you again any time soon."

"You told me I could kick you if you ever took your shit out on me again, and I just took you up on your offer." Heat rushed to my face as I fought my trembling chin and he huffed himself into the cockpit to fiddle with the pilot.

I was horrified that I had struck someone for the first time in my life, but held myself back from rushing to apologize. A deal was a deal.

But we were back on familiar turf now, with tempers appeased and new hope, and we soon spied Gerry's boat on a tack to Cape Sutil. They were so close our short-range Mickey Mouse radio could pick them up, and we made plans for a late supper together. It was late in the afternoon, but we could still troll there through the night bite in a calmer sea, the north end being more protected from the full force of the sou'east wind, and we'd soon picked up a couple dozen coho and a decent-sized spring, the ultimate upper.

As I hummed and gutted the dark-backed coho at the dressing trough, Paul fiddled with something in the checkers after the last pull.

"Hey, I've been thinking about something since the ass-kicking event this morning," he said from the cockpit.

"Oh?" I looked over my right shoulder, acting nonchalant, masking my hope that we might actually talk through something intense instead of ignoring it. He was standing with his back to me, his head tilted back and to one side.

"Yuh, that was weird, you actually kicking me, you know."

"I know and in one way I'm sorry but in anoth . . ."

"I'm not sure I can really trust you anymore."

"What do you mean? That was a tota . . ." I could feel a lump growing in my throat as I turned to face him and laid the knife in the dressing trough.

"I mean . . . I'm gonna have to keep . . . an . . . eye . . . on . . . you . . . from now on." He spun around to face me. A huge sulphur-yellow eyeball was stuck in one of his eye sockets above a monumental grin.

"Jesus, Paul! That's not the snapper's eye, is it? Oh my God, you are totally mental," I shrieked, doubling over the trough with laughter and nearly impaling myself on the dressing knife.

As a grand finale, he scrambled out of the cockpit and started lurching around the deck, arms stretched out in front of him like a zombie, groaning, "I am the ghost of Davy Jones come to thank you for all the fucking gear you've sent me this year. Whooooooooo." Then tried to grab me for a horrible drooly kiss.

"It's a damn good thing you're so cute," I said, kissing his slimy lips.

"Ditto, baby. I think there's more Italian in there than I thought."

"Yeah, well, apparently there's a big dose of Viking in there too."

"Okay, get back to work, show's over, but I'm leaving this here just in case," he said and propped the eyeball up on the hatch cover, looking straight at me. "Oh, uh, by the way, you forgot to dress the spring in the checkers. Jesus, you just can't get decent deckhands anymore." He sauntered back to the cockpit to start pulling in the gear.

This was the first spring he'd let me dress and I turned it into a work of art. When I was done, I dropped it down into the hold and joined him in the cockpit to pull gear, lulled by long, low swells and quiet winds and peaceful, companionable silence.

Suddenly, a powerful intuition told me to look *up*. We were no more than 15 feet away from hitting a boat broadside coming up from our starboard side. Shouting "Paul, wheel," I vaulted out of the waist-high cockpit, over the checkers and across the deck into the wheelhouse. I shut off the pilot and threw the engine in neutral and Paul cranked the wheel. With less than six feet between our poles, we held our breath and watched the other boat troll by, the guy asleep at the wheel . . . literally. Even though he was out cold, he did have right of way, coming from the starboard, and we would have been at fault. If he had come from our left, or portside, we would have had right of way. Not much comfort when you collide four miles offshore with the Coast Guard hours away. Where he came from and how we didn't see him beforehand I never knew, but strangely, we didn't lose one single piece of gear. The last thing I saw was his startled face in the wheelhouse window when we blew the emergency horn after we had passed safely. The gods were having a bit of harmless fun, it seemed.

With the blazing sunset firing up the sky around us we

headed into the familiar landscape of *home* to drop anchor and tie up with Gerry, Steve and little Peter, already waving and smiling from their deck. My heart sang to see them.

After huge hugs all around, I cooked up a scrumptious meal of thick snapper steaks fried in thin pancake batter, mashed potatoes and peas while we hatched a plan to replace the mountain of gear we had lost that morning to keep both our boats running. Paul would hitch a ride from Bull Harbour to Hardy and back over a couple of days; Gerry would run his boat with his six-year-old son, who could already dress fish like a grownup; his deckie, Steve, and I would run ours. I was totally confident I could handle it, as were Paul and Steve. I could barely contain my excitement then or my disappointment when Gerry's Dutch sensibility finally won the day and he offered to *lend* us more gear and help restring the lines the next day in Bull Harbour instead. I loved him dearly for all his caring and generosity, but loved the idea of surprising Paul with a pile of fish I had caught on my own even more.

Taking advantage of the reasonably calm evening, we ran over the bar, which seemed so tame now, and down the channel to slip into Bull Harbour for the peaceful night's sleep we desperately needed. As we crossed the still bay and quietly tied up to a spot on the float, I felt like a college kid come home to Mum and Dad.

"Hey, anybody home?" A familiar, warm voice called from the float with the tap-tap on the hull. I thought I must be dreaming until I heard Paul stir in the day bunk, jump into his jeans and run onto the deck.

"Jesus, Dan, it's great to see you," Paul said, his voice excited as a kid's.

Dan? Oh my God, it couldn't be. We'd heard rumours he had survived the storm from Winter Harbour but weren't sure.

"Oh Dan, I'm so happy to see you," I shrieked, running out to the deck in my flannelette nightie to throw my arms around him, weeping.

"It's okay, Sylvie, I'm all right," he said, hugging me and patting my back. "My boat took a beating, but I got here."

As I hurried to the fo'c'sle to get dressed while Paul made coffee, I heard Dan whisper, "Don't tell her, but I was going to take The Big Jump to get it over with after my poles and mast came down, but something held me back and I just kept going." My eyes filled with tears again and I put my sweatshirt over my mouth to cover my sob as I remembered the sound of his voice whittling away and the crashing rigging and his instructions for where someone could find his love note to his family. But he was alive and here and nothing else mattered and I thanked the gods for sparing him.

Wiping my face dry, I sprinted up the steps, grabbed a coffee and followed the guys down the float to ogle what was left of Dan's boat. It was damn near stripped to the deck. I closed my eyes and took a few deep breaths to still the vertigo—it was a miracle the boat had survived, never mind him. I thought of Dan's wife and kids getting the news from him instead of the Coast Guard.

In Dan's usual sunny way, he said that he'd already set the wheels of insurance in motion and because there was no fire or evidence of foul play, and he wanted to do repairs ASAP and get back out fishing, he would not be accused of framing a *Viking Funeral*, where a fisherman intentionally scuttled or set his boat ablaze for the insurance money. It also helped that the boat had a history of successful seasons and prompt mortgage payments.

Not only was our pal safe and well, but everyone on the floats seemed genuinely happy to see us back home after almost a month on the west coast chasing coho and came by to invite us for coffee—even offered to help Paul and Gerry rewire the gurdies and repair the aerial. Everyone except the managers, who gave us the cold shoulder when we checked in at the office. I suspected they were miffed because we'd sold 17 springs in Hardy instead of here before we left for Winter Harbour for the coho opening July 1.

Paul had justified selling to another buyer for the higher payout because we needed the money so desperately. I didn't agree and had insisted that loyalty was more beneficial in the long run. And now the proverbial chickens had come home to roost. When I bought a few groceries, Pat asked for the money up front instead of just putting it on our tab. On a practical level, we couldn't afford a bad reputation with the camp staff, but they were also good people who had been very kind and helpful to us. Even Paul realized he had blown it when I told him about the grocery bill and gladly left me to the human repair work while he repaired the lines.

I waited until the cramped grocery store/gear shop/fish tally check-in/library/post office was empty and padded across the worn lino past the wooden-plank shelves of tired carrots, tide books, super-hot hoochies and bent-corner detective novels. I leaned through the cut-out window above the counter and spied Pat in the back office at her worn lead-grey metal desk, deep in a pile of fish slips, her hand a blur over the calculator keys. I made a little throat-clearing noise and pulled back to my side of the counter.

"Hi, Pat."

She glanced up from her work with an annoyed look, then a brief softening before shifting to distant.

"Oh, hi. I'm pretty busy here."

"Sorry to bother you. I hoped we could talk for a couple of minutes. Should I come back later?" I nervously fiddled with the bag of jujubes in my hands.

She sighed and looked up again, still distant. "What is it?"

"I guess I just wanted to say that I have a feeling you guys were upset with us for selling our springs in Hardy. I know things are tough for you too, with the fishing being so bad. And I just wanted to say I'm sorry."

"Okay." She shifted back in her seat and turned the old wood swivel chair, her face softening a bit.

"You've all been so good to us, Pat, and we really love it here. I really wish we hadn't sold there. But we had that engine trouble and the pilot thing and Paul just wanted to run straight to Hardy to get things done. I would never want to . . ." I swallowed and swallowed and tried smiling wider to stop the damnable tears from welling up.

"Hey, honey, it's okay." Pat came to the window and put her hand over my clenched fists holding the bag. "I get it. I know you're trying to make things right. He's not a bad guy. A bit of a loose cannon, maybe. None of this can be easy for you." She squeezed my hands gently. "God, you're thin as a stick and I don't like the look of those dark circles under your eyes. You need a time out with the girls."

Pat invited me to cocktail hour in the first-aid room behind the office, an exclusive invitation-only event I'd only heard rumours of before. We whiled away the afternoon with Anne, Pat's daughter-in-law, and a spunky 30-something French–Canadian woman who decked for an inside troller I'd heard over the radio. Sipped gin and tonics, smoked lung-stunning French cigarettes and feasted on smoked salmon and cream cheese on Swedish crackers. Talked about everything from meditation to sailing the Greek Islands to smoking salmon. About home and kids and lovers and dreams for our futures. Laughed and bitched and cried just a bit. I was even offered the use of their state-of-the-art salmon smoker any time I wanted.

Nothing in this world could have nourished me more—mind, body and soul—than those three hours with those fine women in that beautiful place, and we hugged long and hard before wandering back to our business.

Since it was a bit snotty out there, we stayed in another day and ran down to Hardy. We made the most of our harbour time by picking up the pilot we'd dropped off on the Coal Harbour escapade, then had a Chinese supper with pals before begging off a night at the bars to tuck in early. That was before the call for Nurse Sylvia came.

It was always night when the knock came. First the rumble and jolt of voices, sometimes loud and rough with intoxicants, sometimes hesitant and meek with apology. Then the clomp and sway, the clanking and shushing, as they slipped and stumbled aboard, sometimes a pair, sometimes a committee, but never alone. It took gumption to drag a weary deckhand from her bed, to steal those few precious hours of sleep and stillness to come to the aid of a hapless fisherman. Idiots and drunks for the most part, with the occasional innocent thrown in just to remind us of how precarious the fishing life was, how every moment was an opportunity for injury.

I had been a rescuer since I could hold a hand or navigate a Band-Aid. Even though my medical training was a couple of years away yet, it was me they came to, not the first-aid attendant at a camp or the emergency room or doctor in town.

I had already removed my share of hooks, even a halibut hook the size of an anchor, the right way: by cutting the shank with wire cutters and pulling the ends out from either side—usually of hands. Every boat had wire cutters, but not always a first-aid kit and sometimes not even disinfectant.

One night I was hustled to an acquaintance's boat to find his strapping young deckhand shirtless and in shock, drinking straight from a bottle of whiskey at the galley table. My first thought was, *wow, he's even more gorgeous with his shirt off.* Then I snapped out of it when I saw there was something very odd about his chest and the inside of one whole arm—a strange pasty whiteness surrounded by odd little pillows of skin, and around that a fiery red, all of it covered in dark smudges and bits. Even through his fisherman's tan, his face was grey and sweaty.

Turns out he had gone out on a bender and tried to crawl into the upper bunk, lost his balance and fell flat onto the red-hot oil heater. He had seared himself like a steak, and what I saw was a massive area of first-, second- and third-degree burns with grease and toast crumbles embedded in his flesh. I gently took the bottle from his fist, saying that would only make him feel worse later. When I asked for the first-aid kit, there was none, and ours had been cleaned out by the last first-aid event. I had to get the open wounds cleansed and covered fast to avoid a massive infection, knowing full well that he would not go to a doctor or leave the boat.

What they had was a handful of four-by-four gauze pads in sealed packets, and when I asked for vinegar, one of the guys broke the silence by asking me if I was going to pickle him. I said he was pickled quite enough, which sent even Mr. Sirloin Steak into guffaws of relief. I poured the vinegar in the coffee cup I had the skipper scrub out with soap.

For over an hour, I swabbed and scrubbed the grime and crud from him. Then, while he air-dried, I taped the remaining gauze pads together with duct tape and secured the whole apparatus onto his chest and arm 'til he looked like he was wearing body armour. My heart went out to him as he stoically withstood the scouring and the return of feeling in his nerve endings, making the sweat run down his face. Six months later, when that deckhand spotted us on the False Creek wharf back home, he called my name and pulled off his sweater. I couldn't tell which side had been burned.

But that paled by comparison to what I now found in the Port Hardy hotel room Paul and I were driven to at 3:00 a.m. from our boat at the wharf. A bunch of thugs had ganged up on some poor bastard behind the Thunderbird bar a couple of hours earlier and accused him of hustling some chick one of them claimed was his girlfriend. A bystander waded in to pull them off the guy and the nastiest little wharf rat took offense—didn't appreciate the attempt at breaking up the fight, so he bit down hard on the good guy's thumb like a demented pit bull until even his pack tried to pull him off.

Nobody called the cops; nobody wanted trouble. They just brought him to the hotel room and sent someone to collect me. I found him in the bathroom, his hand in the sink, wrapped in a blood-soaked towel, and when I softly said his name he lifted his pallid face, lips trembling in agony. I took a couple of deep breaths and gently unwrapped the mangled mess of his thumb, bitten to the bone, drawing gasps and curses from the men crowding around us. I said he would have to get to the outpost hospital immediately because human bites were the deadliest of any animal's, then went to the room phone and called the local RCMP to get the emergency room opened right away. Something in my voice must have struck a chord, because they sent a car to bring us the few blocks to the hospital. After giving our names and contact info, Paul and I hitched a ride back to the boat with the police and slept as long as the bustling fish camp would let us.

Late the next day, we went to see the patient before leaving to run back to Bull Harbour with our pilot and more gear. The doctor told us it was a good thing we'd done what we did because he would have been dead within a day from the venom of the dirtiest mouth in the world.

After a pit stop in Bull Harbour to set up the pilot and let the sou'east blow itself down a bit, we revved up for a long night run around the top and down to Winter Harbour. We couldn't wait for the morning; we had only 36 hours to get ice and diesel, anchor up behind Kains Island and try to get some sleep before humpback season opened August 1. We had to hit the run hard and fast before it petered out.

"Bring it on," I whispered from my bunk.

For the Living and the Dead

The humpbacks are coming! The humpbacks are coming! And we were ready for them: a pile of new red gear, a hold full of Winter Harbour ice and a pile of cigs, fresh fruit and jujubes for us. All reports said the bulk of the annual run would split at the top of Vancouver Island and come down the outside. That's exactly where we were, anchored up behind Kains Island the night before the August 1 opening, ready to run The Gut with everything working (for once)—pilot, sounder and loran—and an empty bank account hungry for some money.

Since opening July 1, the coho run hadn't been any screaming hell, so the entire trolling fleet was counting on a fish that a few years ago they would have turned up their noses at and left to the ragpickers while they chased the hefty, well-paying springs and sox. But trollers were a practical and adaptable bunch, spending so much time on the seas, and a buck was a buck, which was pretty much what those little humps would be worth that year.

Because humpbacks were the lowest-paying fish of the species, we had to catch a lot to keep our numbers up. They were small and slimy and very hard to dress, especially for big hands.

This made for a very labour-intensive situation with a high potential for belly-cut fish and infected-cut hands. Some fishermen brought their kids on board to dress humps for a couple of weeks until the run moved on, but Paul had my little monkey hands to do the job.

Before dawn on August 1 we picked up the hook behind Kains Island and ran The Gut to join the fleet already forming the mile-square grid pattern 10 miles offshore. I should have been exhausted after 80 days of brutal seas and back-breaking work, but I felt like I was just hitting my stride. I was thinner than I had ever been in my life. Pitiless work had burned the dross from my body, leaving only bone, muscle and sinew— whittled by the wind, scoured by the sea, parched by the sun, pummelled by the relentless rain.

Every cell was attuned to the pitch and roll of the boat as the boom swung and the hooks flew and the guts arranged themselves on the deck in a slimy minefield of fatal falls. If I went overboard I'd die. In 10 minutes I'd be dead from exposure or dragged under by my filling gumboots.

I lost track of what I looked like. Layers of clothing took the place of curves and mounds. That cloudy, cracked little glint above the galley sink could hardly be called a mirror. The best it offered was a mosaic view of myself, and after a while that was just too much trouble and seemed less and less important. Every 10 days or so, I got to hose myself down in a fish-camp shower. It was such a novelty being naked, such a visceral grunt of pleasure.

Day One: 127 fish—17 coho, 110 humps
Day Two: 144 fish—3 springs, 12 coho, 2 sockeye, 127 humps
Day Three: 131 fish—2 springs, 14 coho, 115 humps

And I dressed every damn one of them while Paul pulled and iced, pulled and iced, grabbed a coffee, a strip of Indian Candy, a hunk of cheese.

The weather was spectacular, the seas millpond smooth. We tacked the grid with a hundred other boats, moving in unison, turning in unison, until it was too dark to see. Then we dropped the hook right where we were, still in the grid, scrubbed and cleaned and dressed and iced deep into the night, music loud for those who had none: Men Without Hats to Mozart, Karen Carpenter to Cream. A sea of mast lights reflected a sky of stars. Then the roar of a hundred diesels as everyone began to move: forward and turn and forward and turn and forward and turn.

On the fourth day, the weather and seas turned and we had the best day ever: 111 fish, but 6 were big springs. We ran in to sell to the cash buyer who wanted day-caught fish and paid 10 percent more for them. He paid us $857 in $100 and $50 bills. We held on to the rest of our catch for BC Packers so we could get more ice.

On the fifth day, the weather went lousy and the fish thinned out and so did the boats. Our wash-down pump broke down from running 18 hours a day, so we dressed 60 fish with buckets of water hauled over the side. We heard on the radio that there was some kind of commotion in Bull Harbour and they were looking for new managers, but when the reception went scratchy we could only speculate on what had happened.

I woke up the next morning feeling as dark and jumpy as the weather. We'd lost the fish and were scratching around with a handful of other boats when the call came over the radio telephone. "*Central Isle, Central Isle*, do you read me?" Dan's warm voice sounded tight and strained. Paul went into the cabin to answer and came out a different man.

"Paul, Paul, what's wrong?" I vaulted out of the cockpit and ran to the cabin doorway where he stood trembling and glassy-eyed.

"God, Syl, I don't know how to tell you," he said, passing a hand over his eyes.

"What happened?" I grabbed the bib straps of his Hellys and stared up into his face, my heart pounding. "Is it my parents? My sister? Brother? Who?" I shook his straps to get the thing out of him I didn't want to hear.

"That was Dan. He just came from Bull Harbour. Jesus, Syl, Bob was killed falling into the ice auger two days ago and their son-in-law, Dave, had his arm chewed up and broken real bad trying to rescue him. Christ Almighty, their first clue that something had happened was the red ice coming out of the auger and into someone's hold."

I sagged against him, my head spinning. It wasn't our relatives, but people who had become our family out there. "Oh my God, Paul, we just saw them a week ago. We had drinks with them. They gave us smoked salmon. I can't believe it. Poor Pat. Oh my God. Dave and his wife just got married this spring and she just told me she was pregnant. I can't stand it. That was his father-in-law and his own arm is ruined? God help those poor people."

We held each other tight, wept out our shock and horror. It was always so close, like a shadow creeping behind you. It made no sense. Dan had survived a killing storm for 14 hours; Bob had slipped and fallen; Dave had caught his sleeve. There was nothing left to do but pull in the gear, go in early and pick up the groceries in Winter Harbour that Gerry had radioed us to bring him in Sea Otter Cove. The next day we would go out again.

Most people thought beautiful fish-tailed women lured you into danger, but for us it was a know-it-all old fisherman with a barking German accent that set our teeth and egos on edge. To add to our melancholy over the ice-auger tragedy, the weather was even more miserable and the fish even fewer. So when Mr. Highliner insisted that we too could catch a fortune in fish if we had the balls to come out to *the deep* or *blue water*, Paul took the tantalizing bait and followed the guy's massive steel boat straight out to the distant, dark, almost indigo waters more than 20 miles offshore.

At 75 fathoms and rough seas, we threw out the gear again and caught nothing but Brown Bomber rock cod. Then snarled up our gear while we rolled around for another hour, listening to the old German inform us we must be stupid if we couldn't catch fish that were right under our noses.

We picked up again and kept running out to 100 fathoms while I sat on the hatch cover and watched land speed away from us. My worry-voice whispered—*We are too far from land; this is not safe or good*—as land became a smudgy pencil line and the wind shrieked through our rigging and the waves got jumpier. I tried by sheer force of will to turn the boat around, to override the autopilot. No such luck. Paul was convinced we'd score big if we just kept on the tail of the alleged highliner. But I was familiar with the usual outcomes of these grandiose and often spontaneous schemes.

I couldn't take my eyes off the thinning smudge and felt anxious as a child watching her parent walk away. Paul noticed and said we'd just try it a little while, then turn back. I'd heard that one before too. Now I was bereft and resigned and threw any delusions about long-distance sailing I may have had overboard.

He went into the wheelhouse and emerged a minute later

with a quirky look I couldn't read—it was all in the eyes, the squinchy lips—but I knew I wasn't in trouble about something.

"Go up to the bow," Paul said, and motioned with his head.

"What for?"

"There's something up there you will want to see."

Clinging to the handrail, I crouch-walked up to the fore-deck, finding handholds to keep from pitching over the rearing bow. I had no idea what I was supposed to be looking for and scanned the horizon in exasperation.

"Look down," Paul said through the wheelhouse port window.

And then I saw them. Bullet-shaped grey shadows below the surface, just behind the keel. I couldn't imagine what could swim that fast; we were running at eight knots. I kneeled at the port gunwale and watched the bullets rise to the surface and transform into three silvery dolphins.

"There's more on the other side." He grinned like a kid from the starboard window.

I crept across the bow to see three more bullets speeding along.

"They're riding our wake," Paul said, years falling from his face. "Like surfing."

That explained why they could move so fast—clever little buggers. Not only clever but also gymnastic, as the ones on the starboard side started surging and doing little squiggly leaps in the air. Oddly, the other three were doing exactly the same thing on the other side. I scuttled back and forth like a crab, watching them leap higher and higher, as if competing with each other. Suddenly one of them leapt clear across the bow to the other side, then another and another. I shrieked with delight as they jumped two by two over the bow.

They were the Solid Gold Dancing Dolphins performing their world-famous water ballet. They must have been having the time of their lives, judging from all the clicks and squeals and purrs. My clapping and squealing seemed to egg them on to even greater feats of leaping and gyrating. Then they slowly returned to surfing.

I was shaking and weeping and laughing as I crawled to the port side, where I draped over the gunwale to get closer to those magical creatures. I inched lower and lower and stretched my hand to them, babbled my gratitude and told them how beautiful they were and how much I loved them. One of them slipped onto its side, showed its luminous belly and stared straight up at me, clicking and whirring, as it slowly raised its fin. I reached down, strained to touch, only inches apart, ecstatic. Then I felt a steady pull on my waistband gently hauling me back onto the deck.

"Come on, dolphin girl, I don't want you going overboard with them," Paul said, and steered me back to the hatch cover.

"Thank you, Paul, thank you for showing them to me." I reached up and threw my arms around his neck, pressed my cheek into his rough, woollen sweater.

"I knew you'd get a kick out of them," he said, gently wiping my cheek with his smelly sleeve. "Come on, let's go in. Fuck the blue water and him." He headed for the cabin to turn us around.

Three hours later on the way down the inlet to Winter Harbour, we got a call from Craig in Port Hardy inviting us to the social event of the season: a huge baseball barbecue live-band bash in the park at Stories Bay just outside of town. Craig and his gang of fisher friends, The Wild Ones, were organizing it for the next day, and he announced it was high time we got officially inducted into the gang. He had already invited

Richard and Steve. We could stay on their boat overnight and get a ride back the next day with Craig in his truck from Hardy and his boat from Coal Harbour. All we had to do was hitchhike to Holberg, four or five miles away by logging road, where we would pick up Craig's truck (keys under the mat), which was parked by the general store, and drive to Hardy.

When Paul turned to me with an inquiring face still holding the mic, I yelled, "Yes, we'd love to go!" Craig was a walking upper and just what the doctor ordered to help get us out of our funk. The fishing had dropped off, the weather had turned lousy, and we could pick up a new wash-down pump in town.

As soon as we showered, changed and threw a few things in a bag, we walked out to the road behind the tiny Winter Harbour post office. Minutes later we were picked up by a good-natured logger going back to Holberg in his truck. Above the blasting country-and-western hits, he cautioned us to keep our eyes peeled on this twisty dirt logging road to Hardy where people drove like maniacs and the tree-laden trucks bore down the middle like locomotives.

Now inland, it was hot as stink and we were soon covered in road dust coming in through the truck windows. I chuckled to myself thinking how my mother would rather have walked the 20 miles rather than have one speck of dust touch her perfectly coiffed and heavily lacquered hair. How different her perfect helmet hair was from my unruly mop. I remembered gasping like a guppy with my younger sister and brother in the back of the family station wagon as we drove from Vancouver through the baking heat of the Interior to our cabin property, all the car windows firmly in the upright position.

"Hey, thanks a million for picking us up," Paul said with a bright smile, scooting me in first to sit jammed between them on the dusty, worn bench seat. "I'm Paul and this is Sylvia. We're tied up at BC Packers and going to Holberg to pick up a friend's truck to take to Hardy." He reached across me to shake hands with the bearded, stocky, middle-aged logger.

"No problem. I'm Mike. Good to meet you. Sorry for the junk." He smiled sheepishly at the candy wrappers and pop cans on the floor and jammed a thick bundle of papers and notebooks onto the cluttered dashboard. "I'm one of the foremen at the lumber camp."

"Love the hula dancer." I smiled and pointed to the jiggly dash ornament.

"Got it when the wife and I went to Hawaii last year. She keeps me company on these crazy roads. Sport fishing up here?"

"Nope, commercial. Trollers," Paul said. The dark walls of seemingly endless pine forest pressed close as we vibrated over the washboards and swerved around potholes.

"Heard you guys are having a tough season. That's a shame. Lots of sports stuff starting to go on. The Americans are coming up in droves since their salmon are petering out. Starting to see big cruisers in Ukie and Tofino and I hear there's a big sport fishing business coming into Ucluelet to cater to the Americans, mostly."

"Yuh, I heard he's bringing in 10 or 15 boats that can hold up to five or six people, to rent out or for guided daytrips," Paul said. "I wonder how the government's going to regulate those catches. And there's talk of fish farms going into Alberni Inlet. The Scandinavians have already messed things up with fish farms there, and the government is going ahead with it here. It's crazy."

"I heard about that," Mike said. "Let's hope our government does a better job regulating that stuff here. Fish farms sound like a good idea, but you know what they say about things being too good to be true. Where did you say your friend's truck was?"

Mike drove us right to the truck, wished us good fishing and a fine time in Port Hardy, and drove away with a wave and a shave-and-a-haircut-two-bits honk.

We hightailed it to Port Hardy over more dirt road, nearly driving into the bush to avoid two loaded logging trucks, and were thankful to hit town roads again. We wandered the government wharf and found Richard's boat and a cheery welcome. I repaired Steve's haircut, which Richard had given him with a weed whacker, and after a tearful recount of the ice-auger nightmare, we sauntered up to the Seagate for greasy fries, burgers and slightly skunky beer. I savoured every disgusting bite and swallow.

An old bearded gent sat alone a few tables away, an island of solitude in the middle of the smoky caterwauling, sipping his beer and gazing at something beyond the dingy walls and this frontier town clinging to the edge of the wilds. With soft-spoken dignity, he accepted our offer to join us for a beer. We wheedled a few stories: grappling with grizzlies, sewing a fingertip on backwards, burying his young bride and baby behind a sod hut. He had trapped and dogsledded and gold panned from Alaska to Yukon and Northwest Territories and down to the wilds of northern Oregon. He never met my eyes or answered my questions, so I let the men draw the magic from him before he quietly rose and thanked us for our generosity and walked straight-backed into the night.

Demurely refusing Richard's offer of his double bunk, Paul and I chose to spend the last currency of our energy on a night of passion and deluded privacy in the luxury of a real bed with dry sheets in a room that didn't move. Besides, the infamous *Kelly*

Ruth had tied up to Richard's boat and every ho and drunk in town would be partying on the boat that was known all over the coast for its painted penis *K* and lolling-tongued Rolling Stones mouth on the cabin sides.

These were partiers the likes of Mad Dog, who, a few months ago, the RCMP had chased driving a hundred miles an hour on the treacherous road from Port Alberni to Ucluelet—we and the rest of the bar had watched him drive off the pier and into Ucluelet Inlet. When Mad Dog's head broke the surface, cigarette still clenched between his teeth, he gave the cops the finger and shouted, "You'll never take me alive, ya dirty screws," before turning onto his belly and swimming across the inlet to the Native village, Ittatsoo, where the cops couldn't nab him. What finally caught him was a gas leak on his fishboat that blew him to kingdom come when he lit a cigarette and burned his boat to the waterline—just the way he would have wanted it.

The Wild Ones were tame by comparison. After a logger-sized breakfast at the local diner and buying a new wash-down pump and a pair of dove-grey cords to replace the pants that now hung off me, we hopped a ride with Richard and Steve's friend out to the party of the decade. Hundreds of people converged by land and sea on the paradise of a park 10 miles out of town on a long, silvery beach that looked over the strait and small islands. A gaggle of boats, from massive steel draggers to sleek little pleasure rockets, bobbed at anchor in the sparkling bay, their skiffs filled to the gunwales with goodies and merrymakers all racing for shore like seals after salmon. Vehicles of every vintage filled the dirt parking lot and lined the two-lane roads as far as you could see. Fisherfolk and loggers and miners and townies with their kids and dogs. Pickups loaded with sawhorses and two-by-fours, tables and barbecues. Everyone laughing and busy and buzzing with excitement as the white-chalked baseball diamond emerged and the stage grew strong and the generators and electric cables powered up the speakers and strung lights looping around the stage. A monster tape deck pounded out everything from Led Zeppelin to Patsy Cline, as everyone pitched in to create a cross between Woodstock and a Sunday church picnic. Some of the bigger fellas kept an eye on the young bucks and drinkers and waltzed them out when they got a bit wrangy, which was less often than at any big-city bar I'd been in. Someone brought balloons and popcorn for the kids, who spun like tops in the old school playground. A marathon of baseball games and a potluck seafood barbecue, picnic tables loaded with every edible imaginable. In the early evening, as some of the young families made for home, a pretty decent local rock band kept everyone dancing into the night, until Wes the heavy hitter quietly came on stage and a roar went up from the massive crowd.

Wes had run with all the Big Dogs of blues—Muddy Waters, John Lee Hooker, Stevie Wonder, Bo Diddley—and had found his way here from South Carolina a few years previous. Nobody knew how or why he appeared in Port Hardy. He kept to himself and led a quiet life working for the township during the day, teaching guitar at night and playing in the local pubs once in a blue moon. But when he cranked out those three Bo Diddley hits, everyone was up on their feet dancing and clapping and singing at the top of their lungs.

We danced all night under the stars and big-bellied moon, barefoot in the cool, fresh grass that filled us up with life and joy. We owed it to the living and to the dead.

Home

It was so easy to ignore Gaia's whispers that autumn was coming, with the land and sea awash with golden light, the winds gentle and warm, and all her creatures languorous in the late summer days. But the signs came early in the north: the taste of the wind, the cast of the sun, the burnished look of the land. Northern summers are counted in weeks, not in months like the south. The farther north you go, the more compressed and intense summer becomes, the light pushing hard into the night, fighting for every moment until giving way to relentless winter.

As the lucky and the strong made their way past the fleet to their Mother Streams, the last of the stragglers were brought on board, a few dozen a day, to help feed the world and make another boat mortgage payment. We played out the last days of August and into September in long, slow sweeps back and forth from the north-end Yankee Spot through Cape Scott to Cape Cook, selling in Winter Harbour or Port Hardy. But never again to Bull Harbour. We just couldn't bring ourselves to stand in that office or watch the ice rush down that auger. Nothing against the new people—we'd heard they were very nice.

We often sold our day catches to the Neptune cash buyer outside Winter Harbour and even picked up extra ice for free from the other camps because they liked us and everything seemed to be winding down, the fierceness of it all melting away in the slanting sun and fog that had started drifting in more often.

I never got used to being offshore in that strange, muffled world of west coast fog so thick we couldn't see our own bow. One thick morning, an old-timer on the radio informed his pal that he was hanging up because he had to go on deck to sweep the fog off his bow so he could see where he was going.

There was a lot more entertaining radio chit-chat going on. By that point, whatever season you were going to have was had, and people who'd had a lousy season, which was most everyone, were just trying to extend their time by a few more weeks to accumulate enough stamps to apply for Unemployment Insurance benefits and hope to God the claim was processed by Christmas. So fisherfolk might as well relax and have a few laughs over the non-stop comedy coming over the airwaves. Since the competition for fish was pretty much done, they competed to outdo each other with outrageous stories and superstitions.

Like the ragpicker who pulled a massive halibut into his stern that proceeded to smash the shit out of everything, including the fisherman, who panicked after not being able to gaff it to death and decided to shoot it with a handgun he kept in his cabin. Good news was he killed it before it totally destroyed his net and drum; bad news was the bullet passed through the halibut's head *and* the deck *and* the hull.

Then came a load of El Niño stories. No one really understood that weather phenomenon, that weird warming of the ocean surface that arises at Christmas off the western coast of South

America. The cold nutrient-rich water doesn't well up, which causes die-offs of plankton and fish and alters Pacific currents and storm tracks and even reverses trade winds, disrupting weather around the world. Stories more fantastical than the last about weird and wonderful creatures that came up with the tropical waters every four or five years. Acres and acres of silver-dollar-sized luminous jellyfish that travelled on the surface of the ocean by the small sails on their backs. They'd come into the boat on the lines and gear, and if touched, they left an invisible acid so strong it burned your skin and could only be neutralized with baking soda. The howls of barehanded greenhorns innocently peeing over the side could be heard for miles. Locals caught tuna off the dock in Zeballos, an inland mining town 50 miles up a twisting inlet, when tuna were normally chased 200 miles offshore. The six-foot circular sunfish, flat and pale as a piece of plywood, caught outside of Prince Rupert, another 300 miles north of Cape Scott. The fish mounted on the wall of the old Savoy Hotel, scene of many a frontier debauchery, before a blaze turned everything to ash.

El Niño wreaked havoc with the West Coast trollers. Especially with sockeye, the troller's meal ticket, when the fish would disappear altogether from the warmer outside waters and run for the colder water of the Inside Passage. It devastated trollers who had only outside licences. The warm water also brought in huge schools of mackerel that loaded the lines so trollers couldn't catch anything else and ate every salmon smelt in sight, dramatically reducing future runs of mature salmon—a double whammy.

It was all so complex and interconnected—what the eco-activist Dr. David Suzuki, the ethnobiologist Dr. Wade Davis and the Greenpeace environmental warriors called The Web.

Even scientists didn't really know what made salmon tick, never mind what affected this mythic fish that had been the lifeblood of coastal peoples for thousands of years. We knew more about living in space than we did about the life cycle of salmon.

Then came the rehashing of old seagoing superstitions to explain the epidemic of poor catches, engine breakdowns, lost gear, bad injuries, running aground. But how could opening a can upside-down or changing a boat name bring havoc, or throwing salt over your shoulder or putting a coin under the mast save you from disaster? I reasoned my way through the ancient taboo against women on long sailing-ship voyages and working boats—it could get a little tricky out there with a boatload of randy sailors.

The superstition was so serious in old Britain that if a woman even stepped foot on a boat, the men would have it scrubbed stem to stern and exorcised by a priest, or even scuttled, rather than go out to sea on it, especially the dories of Northern Scotland that fished the treacherous North Sea. The fishing museums in tiny towns all along the Scottish coasts bore witness to the outcome of many a deadly trespass. On the Firth of Forth, a bronze statue of a Fishwife stood on the shore of an ancient fishing village, eternally looking out to sea, eternally waiting, just as women were meant to be . . . until the last wee while. But for most of us out here, man or woman, there was someone somewhere who waited and wondered and worried.

The local First Nations people had their own myths and legends, of a much nobler intent, about personal integrity and how to conserve salmon for future—something the modern world had fallen back on a day late and a buck short.

The Haida told of a great shining, leaping fish that each year brought big medicine to the village of the Great Chief and his people, a life-giving creature his daughter had seen in a dream. In the time when people and animals were the same beings, four supernatural brothers came to the Squamish to help them find the village of the Salmon People and convinced the fish people to come every year to the Squamish. Chief Spring Salmon promised he would send these fish in order from the early spring to the fall: the spring salmon, sockeye, coho, dog salmon, then humpback. They would come for all eternity to feed the people as long as the fish were honoured and their bones carefully gathered and returned to the sea. The Yakima told a legend about when the salmon disappeared because the people ignored the Creator's warning about protecting them. All the people's attempts to revive the salmon failed until the great Sea Snake took pity and used his powers to restore them.

But these dire warnings and rumours of recession and declining stocks were a million miles away that day as we lounged and laughed and even danced on the deck between pulls in our gumboots and Hellys. Two songs became our anthem, the hottest hits in the north-end fleet, played over and over. We could see people bobbing around in their sterns or shouting out about feelin' fine and peace of mind, groovin' to "Draggin' the Line" by Tommy James and the Shondells or to the hard-luck guts and glory of "Fishing Grounds" by Ken Hamm, a Canadian blues legend living on Vancouver Island.

Nothing else mattered but being here in this glorious place, being gloriously free to go gloriously broke. Sure we had to make a living, but it was so much more than that—each in our own way was answering the call of the wild. Some more renegade, more educated, more spiritual, more rough-around-the-edges than others, but we were all members of an ancient tribe that had already begun its descent along with a way of life that would soon be lost to the world. And I would hold that fierce glory in my heart forever.

As we motored into Fisherman Bay that night with the biblical sky unfolding around us, Paul steering, his arm around my shoulders, me leaning against him, my arm around his back, my eyes filled with tears.

"What's up?" he said gently, tilting my chin up toward him. "You okay?"

"This is the most romantic moment of my life."

"On a dirty, old fishboat, with a dirty, old fisherman, after not having a shower for a week? You are one strange chick," he laughed, squeezing me to him.

"No, I mean it, Paul. There's something so powerful and beautiful about this. This is what humans have been doing for half a million years, a bonded pair out in the natural world together fighting for survival to make a life for themselves and relying on each other for even their life and safety. Especially with the dirty and smelly and dangerous. How many people get to do this together anymore? We're like a dying breed, people who work together, and I will always be thankful that I got to do this and share it with you."

"You're something else, that's for sure," he said, and kissed the top of my head. "C'mon, let's get the anchor down. I want to check the engine. It seems to be vibrating a little. I think we should troll toward Goletas just in case. I don't want to get stuck in the middle of nowhere if something goes wrong."

By the time we hit the channel we could feel a definite vibration coming through the floor. We started to run for Hardy with another fog bank chasing us all the way. An hour out of Hardy Bay the fog engulfed us just as the engine temperature started to climb. The *Central Isle* limped into the harbour with steam belching through the floor, and coasted to the closest float of the commercial wharf.

It was over. The engine was shot without even a chance of a Viking Funeral, and we sat up all night trying to decide how we would deal with this wretched end to our season. Engine repairs would eat up most of what we'd saved after accounting for the mortgage payments. There would be no school this year. The best I could do was go home to Vancouver, find a job and a place for us to live while Paul stayed in Port Hardy to fix the engine and then bring the boat home. Later he could try to lease a gillnetter for the fall runs. He had been an ace gillnetter before trading the nets for hooks two years before. I prayed he'd be able to make up for our loss.

Then the phone calls, collect, to everyone I cared about and some I didn't. Dialled from the graffiti-covered booth at the top of the wharf next to the clanging of the forklifts and the grinding of the ice auger, awash with bittersweet responses of relief and disappointment: *Yes, I'm fine. No, I didn't make any money. Yes, we're still together. No, he won't be coming home quite yet. Yes, I need to find a job. No, I can't live at the house. Yes, it was worth it. No, I don't hate him. Yes, I am very thin. No, I can't wait to settle in court. Yes, we are going to live together. No, I don't regret it. Yes, I want to see Gay's baby. No, I haven't forgotten my family. Yes, you're still my best friend in the whole world. No, I didn't get hurt. Yes, I need a place to stay for a couple of weeks. No, I'm not lying. Yes, I missed you. No, I won't go back to you. Yes, I've changed. Yes, I feel good. Yes, I feel bad. Yes, I wish it had turned out different. Yes, I'm sure.*

Paul and I were careful and kind with each other in those last hours together, quietly going about our business, buffering ourselves and our fledgling relationship forged in the crucible of the last four months. I'd return home as I'd left, broke and homeless, but altered to my core and without a molecule of regret. No matter how tough things would get, I had a new benchmark for endurance and profound experience that would never be bested.

I had chosen life again and always would.

I left Port Hardy on a Greyhound bus at dawn, waving good-bye to the man I had despised and adored as intensely as I had everything else in that world. That I'd already shared more with than many people do in a lifetime. As the hours and miles rolled by, a stream of images played out in reverse on the window: eagles on the mud flats, schools of islands, totems guarding a broken beach, brilliant worlds clinging to pylons. Then the cars, and more cars, and trucks and stoplights. Hamlets became villages, then towns: Port McNeill, Kelsey Bay, Campbell River, Courtenay, Qualicum, Parksville. Faster and faster, louder and louder, then the mill town of Nanaimo and the ferry terminal that I'd driven through a thousand times, now overwhelming with traffic and noise and unnatural smells. Past the lighthouses and markers and buoys, south and more south, from the fishing grounds 400 miles away. Then the blessed relief of the Strait of Georgia on the massive *Queen of Tsawwassen* ferry, crossing the calm inside waters on the incoming tide. Past the deep-sea freighters tethered in Burrard Inlet to the sheltered Horseshoe Bay terminal and its charming urban village. Then swept up by my best friend Beenie in a flurry of hugs and kisses and tears; our time apart felt like four days or 400 years. A thousand stories, a million words and no idea where to start but to cry and laugh.

Along the sinuous highway that hugged the mountainous shoulders of Vancouver. More cars, more buildings, more tears of reunion, then the first sight of my beautiful, brash city. The tape deck blasting Steely Dan while Beenie made plans for a night of sushi at the Asahi and carousing at the Ankor.

My body was strapped into Beenie's little beater, but my heart and spirit had yet to find me in this kaleidoscope of old and new. I murmured absently as she burbled about what I looked like and how I'd changed. Across Burrard Inlet and my last look at the sea from the Lions Gate Bridge. Through the erotic clamour of downtown Vancouver to False Creek that rippled into the salty heart of the city. To a glittering tower where I gazed down on the blue-collar corner of the Granville Island boat basin that I'd left from on that pussy-willow morning a lifetime ago.

Epilogue

I am where I have been so many times before: alone on a wind-swept beach. I always know what to do here. I always know who I am here. This is no technicolour Tahitian dream beach— it is Canada's wild western coast, my home, my lifeblood. I am soaked to the marrow with it and can't live without it. Every cell of me sighs with relief.

The land and sea have gifted me with a perfect moon shell. I have found others, but they are broken. I almost discard them but glance again and realize that if they were not broken, I could not see the symmetry and beauty of the design, the perfect and elegant spiralling to the centre.

I am in a paradise of cedar and sand and wind and waves and fresh, rushing water. Hunkered down in a little trailer so much like a boat, beside a stream under the cedar trees in Powell River, a sturdy town on BC's Sunshine Coast. The sun flashes its most engaging smile. The stream flings itself to the sea. The gods have conspired to seduce a book out of me.

On the ferry from Vancouver, I had stood transfixed in front of the gift-store bookrack. My colleague who is here with me to mentor and teach the emerging Powell River writers said, "This is where your book will be." I wanted to see it there so bad it tugged at my guts.

During a drizzly Vancouver winter in 2006, I fled to Arizona to write a historical novel about the northern BC coast and the people who made their living on the sea. That didn't happen. I sat for two days with six months of research strewn about me, completely blocked. In desperation I started writing about my own experiences in that world in the mid-1980s, thinking they would stream me into the novel. The novel never happened, but the stories insisted on themselves and became portholes into the world I lived in as a young woman, deckhanding in the commercial salmon trolling fleet.

The stories shouted and laughed and wept their way out of me as I sat baking in the desert. They dragged me mercilessly through those months at sea. Pulled me down into whirlpools of memory and then threw me back on shore blinking and shivering. To find myself deep in the Southwest desert instead of the Northwest waters. I came home with 30,000 words of life stories that sang like sirens on the rocks.

Now, four years later, I had arrived at the Willingdon Beach Campsite in Powell River. Soon after I settled in, the camp manager's wife came by and asked if I'd like to feed the fish. I followed her upstream, a few feet from my door, to a 20-foot trough, similar to a culvert cut in half lengthwise and covered with metal catwalk lids that she raised to reveal 70,000 humpback salmon fry. I fed them in fanned handfuls from a recycled ice cream bucket, a dry granular stuff that looked like coffee grounds and smelled like dead seal. The quicksilver babies boiled to the surface for supper.

Quietly beside myself, I asked if she knew why I was there. She said no, that my colleagues hadn't said, just that I would be staying for a few days. I told her I had come from Vancouver to teach and edit at the annual Powell River Writers' Conference and work on my book about the salmon-fishing industry. She smiled and shook my hand and welcomed me to town, reminded me that Powell River was a thriving hotbed of the arts.

She said the babies had arrived the night before by Department of Fisheries and Oceans truck. They would be nurtured for about three weeks until they doubled in size, to three inches, before being released into the stream to rush out to sea a hundred feet away to continue their life cycle. The stream water was piped into the nursery trough to imprint the smell of home on the babies. Another 55,000 larger smolts in a submerged seawater tank at the end of the breakwater in a float dock would be released into the ocean in a few days. As many as Man and Nature allowed would come back to their Mother Stream in 18 months by smelling their way home through hundreds of Pacific miles. Fisheries hoped 40 percent of the babies, about 50,000 fish, would return home to spawn. Much fewer would.

In a simple gesture of nurturance and stewardship, campsite guests pitched in to feed the babies, to do their part to help curb the devastation we have wrought on this planet.

A similar nurturance draws a gathering of wordsmiths to the writing conference. I love them for their courage and tenacity; I know in my bones that I'm on my mark and doing what I love: inspiring people to believe the writing life is real and doable. For 12 years I have supported the literary communities of British Columbia through my involvement with the Federation of BC Writers, first as a regional director on the board, then as president and finally as chief administrator. I have encouraged writers to manifest their passion in literary events and writing programs throughout North America. Coached, edited and consulted with authors and entrepreneurs around the world. Written hundreds of articles and short stories. Everything I ever learned or did, every career I thrashed through, from engineering to counselling to teaching, every thought or feeling or philosophy I ever had, has funnelled into what I do now.

For four years I have shared *The Fisher Queen* stories, from Haida Gwaii to Arizona, conferences to coffee shops, radio to ranches—even made shortlist for the CBC National Literary Awards in 2010 with the Great Grey Beast story. People crowded into reading rooms, flocked to literary events, asking, *When will these stories be a book?* Their faces lit with the longing to know and touch another tile in the great mosaic of this country and how the Wild West informs who we are.

Electric energy crackles any time creative minds and diligent focus come together. This little-engine-that-could of a conference is no exception. The air in the room where I teach my master class hums with the high hearts and hard work of going pro in the writing world. At noon, a motley crew of presenters and organizers and attendees thankfully piles into cars for the windy drive through Powell River's business district, past the devolving pulp mill and to the town limits, where we will lunch and absorb the expanse of lake and tree and sky to fuel us through the indoor hours. Coasties can't be away from the wilding world for long before things start coming undone inside us.

We are randomly arranged at four long tables set end to end along the windows: locals on one side, facing in, guests on the other, facing out. It's hard to be completely present when the wind and water are tugging me to come join them. It's hard to pay attention when my eyes follow the weavings of the eagles, when my nose catches the edge of the sea. The quiet woman across the table is watching me; the chatty woman next to her repeats something.

"I am so glad we came to your class this morning, I had a feeling it would be really good and you were great. My friend didn't even want to come, but I dragged her here. I just had a feeling we really needed to be here and I'm so glad we came. It was so interesting. I kept telling her—oh, I'm Joan and this is Anne, by the way; you remember us, right?—I kept telling her something really great might happen and maybe she'd get inspired to write."

"I don't write, at least not up to now," the quiet one says with a faint smile.

"I'm so glad you came," I say, and something about her makes me really mean it.

"Someone told us you used to be a deckhand on a salmon boat and you are writing about it. That's amazing. Anne used to work in the salmon-fishing industry too, right, Anne?"

"That's amazing, Anne, it's a pretty small sisterhood," I say, encouraging her to reveal more. The faint smile reaches her distant grey eyes and she simply agrees.

It starts out normal enough: we learn I worked on a salmon troller, she worked in a fish camp; I was a full-on deckhand and cabin slave, she was a bookkeeper and first-aid attendant; I fished with my boyfriend, she worked for BC Packers.

"In Bull Harbour? Oh my God, we fished out of there all the time!" My words rush and tumble. "In the 1980s? That's when I was there. Did you work with Dave and his wife? The guy that died in the ice auger? And you were the first-aid attendant?"

When she says yes and that she remembers our boat and fixes me with those searchlight eyes, a high wind rushes through me. It's hard to hear her, but I see her lips say, "I thought it was you."

"My God, you are in my book. Oh my God, I know who you are." My heart races and it's hard to breathe, a dark green mountain wave rushes toward me—I just have to hang on to the wheel and keep the bow pointing into it. The world telescopes down to this electric conduit that connects us and sends us spinning 25 years back in time. I watch myself slowly lift my arms and extend my hands to her across the table, palms down. I feel a trickling on my face and don't know why my eyes are blurry.

I hear myself say in a bright voice untouched by 25 years of full-calamity living: "It's me, the little girl with the broken hands." Some small part of me knows how surreal this seems to those near us, but I can only keep the bow pointing into the wave and pushing forward. She says she knows. I ask her if she remembers what she did for me. She does. I watch a silver track slide down her pale cheeks.

Her friend is weeping. "When I said I dragged her here because I knew something was going to happen here, I meant it. She has breast cancer, just diagnosed before we came here. I told her that maybe if something inspired her to write, even in a journal, it would help her."

I turn to those eyes that had noticed the festering wounds I had tried to hide, those hands that had tended mine, that mouth that had comforted me through the terrible pain. Those arms that had held and rocked me in that tiny plank-board room that smelled of disinfectant and fish guts as I sobbed my fear and loneliness.

"You saved my life 25 years ago and maybe we're here for me to return the favour. Maybe something today will help shift what is happening inside your body." I slowly come back into mine and the room around me. Everything has gone very still and quiet except for the faint gasps and sniffs.

They say that we barely spoke above a whisper, that a casual observer enjoying the view from across the room would hardly have noticed. But those at our table said they were changed forever, each to their own need, by what they had witnessed. Exchanged serendipity for coincidence, perhaps even considered the possibility of a grander plan.

Every time Anne and I passed each other in the bustle of the conference activities, I asked, "Did that really happen?"

And she would say, "Yes, little sister, it did, every bit of it. It's time to tell the story."

I will forever be deeply connected to how the land and sea talk to us. I will always know when *something* is coming. I'll look up and scan the skies and sniff the wind, on a wild mountaintop or a frenetic cityscape, and murmur that it's shifted to slack, get ready for it. Those who know me will pay attention.

The Wild West has gone to its condos and fish farms, yet still nature insists on being heard. I am older, plumper, shrewder and a little road weary, but my gypsy soul still leaps and flings its irreverent laugh all about the place.

I went to sea and met my Sisiutl. Faced my horror, faced my fear and answered the call that drew me through my journey home to the Mother Stream that is me.

Afterword

Humans have always harvested the land and seas to feed themselves and the world. Now we must feed seven billion of us. In 40 years, there will be many more to feed, and we must increase our food production by twice as much. Fishers are among the last hunter-gatherers in the world and fish are among the last wild food. And the greatest of those fish on Canada's west coast is the mighty salmon.

For millennia, five species of wild salmon have been inextricably woven into the tapestry of life in the Pacific Northwest. One of the rare fishes that lives in both fresh and salt water, salmon's rich, dense and delicious flesh, loaded with life-sustaining nutrients and oils, is prized by both animals and humans. For the fish, the oils allow them to survive migration for thousands of miles and the final powerful push to reach their inland spawning grounds, fighting their way against the current, often through predators, rapids and shallows.

During their life cycle, wild salmon carry nutrients from river to sea and back again—as living food and then as fertilizer after they spawn, die and decompose. Salmon have provided humans with not only an integral food but also a foundation for Pacific Northwest culture, and for 5,000 years have been a cornerstone of wealth and commerce. Only in the last 200 years has that ancient balance been disturbed and rocked to its core as competition for this dwindling resource becomes more and more fierce.

The First Nations people of the Pacific Northwest were the first commercial trollers on the BC coast, fishing in small dugouts and using baited hooks with hand-pulled lines. While they braved the wild coastal weather and waters, inland tribes braved the powerful currents of the Fraser, Thompson and Stikine Rivers, trapping and harvesting the returning adult salmon in complex weirs owned by clan families. Fish were dressed and dried to sustain villages throughout the winter. Especially for inland peoples, poor runs meant starvation.

In May 1670, King Charles II of England signed the charter for his nephew Prince Rupert that created the Hudson's Bay Company (HBC) and changed the fate of the BC salmon fisheries and Canadian resource allocation forever. The company was granted unrestricted dominion over "the sole Trade and Commerce of those seas . . . with Fishing of all sorts of Fish, Whales, Sturgeon and all other Royal Fishes in the Seas, Bays, Inlets, and Rivers within the Premises."

When Alexander Mackenzie explored the Fraser River in 1793, he was stunned by the enormous numbers of salmon moving upstream and filled his canoes daily to sustain his crew. By 1808, Simon Fraser had begun the first trade in salmon with local First Nations on the lower Fraser River, noting the phenomenal harvest by "means of barriers" and the people's relative wealth.

Those ancient traditions would change dramatically in 1827 with the building of Fort Langley, the HBC trading post, 30 miles upstream from the mouth of the Fraser River on BC's southwest coast. As the first commercial salmon fishery grew exponentially, Native men provided tens of thousands of fish annually while Native women cleaned, salt-cured and packed the catch in barrels for shipping to Hawaii, then on to Asia and South America to an exploding salt-fish market.

The Fraser Canyon Gold Rush in 1858 saw an estimated 30,000 prospectors pass through Victoria to pan the river, and clashes with Native communities soon followed. Over 2,000 Babine peoples arrived at their ancestral river fishing grounds north of Yale to find an environmental catastrophe: clear-cutting, stream diversion, destroyed gravel spawning beds. The ensuing conflict left fish camps destroyed and 31 Native villagers, including chiefs, dead. Eventually an uneasy deal was struck, and by 1906 the Department of Indian Affairs reached an agreement with the Babines that in return for dismantling their weirs and in lieu of land claims, they would be given nets for food fishing and trade.

As the Industrial Revolution erupted in England, the BC fish-canning industry was launched in 1871 by Alexander Ewen to feed the masses of hungry factory workers. Thirty thousand one-pound tin cans were hand-soldered and hand-filled with 2,000 sockeye in 300 cases. Nine years later, 42,000 cases were shipped; just one year later, over 120,000 cases. Sockeye were prized over other salmon species, even the magnificent spring salmon, because of their superior quality for canning. Pulling in up to a thousand fish at a time, the fishers tossed everything but sockeye, consider-ing the other fish garbage and not worth hauling, and left a trail of dead salmon behind them as they rowed to shore.

Canneries admitted to discarding up to 3,000 fish plus guts and offal into the tidal waters at the mouth of the Fraser River every day, which many people saw as the cause of typhus epi-demics that raged through the fledgling city of Vancouver and outlying villages.

By 1900 there were more than 1,000 canneries on the BC coast, employing mostly Native and Chinese workers. By 1913 cannery-employed multi-national fishers (Scandinavians,

Greeks, Italians, Englishmen, Frenchmen, Chileans and Hawaiians) used hand-pulled linen nets or handlines from 20-foot rowing skiffs. Each dawn they went out and pulled in the massive catches that sent 2.3 million cases of salmon around the world in 1900. A fisher earned $2.25 for a 12-hour shift and a rower earned $1.00; a crude tent slung across the bow and a cut-down oilcan stove was their only comfort.

But early one August morning in 1913, a catastrophic event in the Fraser Canyon destroyed 75 percent of the sockeye run and decimated the industry for the next 80 years. Some say forever. As Canadian Northern Railway crews blasted tunnels through the canyon, a rockslide sent 76,000 cubic metres of debris into the Fraser River at Hells Gate and narrowed the river into a destructive torrent. Millions of sockeye were wiped out in one of the biggest environmental disasters in BC history. Only by the heroic efforts of First Nations people with dip nets and baskets carrying live fish upstream over the slippery rocks and of federal fisheries officers frantically dredging and building wooden box flumes were a few thousand sockeye saved. The Fraser did not bear salmon again until the Hells Gate Fishways opened in 1945.

In 1917 Canada and the United States formed the International Pacific Fisheries Commission to improve salmon runs to spawning beds—in some cases, hundreds of miles inland. Over the years, this joint commission has built fishways—artificial channel systems of low steps (or ladders) that help salmon through the difficult sections of the Fraser River system—at Yale, Hells Gate and Bridge River Rapids. In 1941 only 1,100 fish reached the spawning beds in the BC Interior Quesnel Lake system; by 1973 the number had increased to over 250,000 fish, and in 1981 to over 800,000. But 30 years of significant scientific planning and several years of construction still have not completely repaired the damage done a century ago.

By the early 1920s, gasoline-powered trollers with multiple lines from V-shaped trolling poles began to appear, and in the 1930s, holds were filled with ice to allow for trips of several days farther offshore. By the 1960s, freezing systems extended trips even further. By the 1980s the BC troll fleet consisted of 1,600 freezer, ice and day boats. However, by the year 2000, the fleet was downsized to 544 boats as part of a government buyback and licensing scheme.

When the first reports of salmon-stock depletion on the BC coast filtered back to Ottawa in the 1880s, federal fisheries responded to environmental and resource concerns. They made fishing licences mandatory in 1894, and made trap nets and purse seines illegal. That decision was rescinded a few years later under pressure from fishers in competition with lower-cost American producers. Native weirs had already been banned and land claims pushed to the back burner, leaving many First Nations disgruntled. Canneries were lobbying for more power. Fishers and cannery workers were striking and forming unions. Dissension among fishers grew as various factions of net fishers and hook fishers saw each other as market competitors.

The stage was set for decades of escalating tensions and conflict, as user groups demanded their voices be heard and their share be given. Commercial sport fishing, fish farming, international fishing rights, industrial pollutants, habitat destruction and environmental and climatic change have turned the industry into a many-headed Hydra. Each user group loudly defends itself while blaming others for dwindling stocks, accusing each other of greed and mismanagement. What makes management even more complex is that salmon are migratory, moving through Canadian,

American, Russian and Japanese waters. In response, the 1985 Canada–United States Pacific Salmon Treaty and the 1992 North Pacific Anadromous Fish Commission treaty signed by Japan, Canada, Russia and the United States were created to manage collective research and eliminate destructive practices like high-seas drift nets and trafficking of illegally caught salmon.

The Canadian government, through its Department of Fisheries and Oceans, now known as Fisheries and Oceans Canada, has answered these challenges primarily through licensing and regulations, environmental measures and salmon-enhancement programs. Regulations regarding season length, timed openings, gear and area restrictions, quotas, non-retention and allocation limits extend to all gear types (hook, net and drag).

Unfortunately, each group often feels it is being unfairly burdened with regulations and therefore lobbies for leniency, as trollers did after being restricted to a four- to six-week annual season and increasingly reduced fishing areas.

Beginning as a school project in North Vancouver, the extensive federally funded Salmon Enhancement Program was launched in the late 1970s to support recreational and commercial fisheries and to rebuild depressed stocks. Despite 19 BC hatcheries producing and releasing an average of 485 million salmon fry and smolts, only a small fraction of them, about one percent, returned to spawn. Whether the high mortality rates are from industrial pollutants, disturbed spawning grounds, rising ocean temperatures, unreported over-fishing, diseases and parasites from farmed fish or a combination of all of these is still unclear.

The rise of the commercial sport fishery, which is seen by other user groups as the *sexy* fishery and the darling of the regulators, is a relatively modern phenomenon. Not to be confused with the personal recreational sport, where folks catch a fish or two for their own table, these major commercial ventures range from exclusive lodges to small charter boat operators who cater to a largely well-heeled crowd seeking adventure holidays.

It was completely unregulated until 1951, when a daily limit came into effect, and personal sport fishing licences came 30 years later. In an industry still largely unregulated and run by volunteers, sport fishermen are now required to purchase an annual licence and adhere to catch limits. Boat totals are reported by the honour system, though many people believe that commercial sports operations should be as closely regulated as commercial fisheries.

Some sources say sport fishers take only three percent of the annual take, but others, especially commercial fishers, say that number is grossly inaccurate, and stories of illegally caught, canned, frozen and sold fish run rampant. Sport fishers are also not required to adhere to any closures or other restrictions, giving them priority access to springs and coho and protecting the fishery from changes in abundance.

Seen as a key element in BC's recreational and commercial well-being, commercial sports operations are significantly tied to the tourist industry. In the 1960s sport fishers began to organize to protect their interests and created the Fishing Advisory Board, which now represents the interests of several hundred thousand anglers and business owners.

By far the most controversial and volatile issue on the BC coast is fish farming. The answer to world hunger to some people, environmental holocaust to others, fish farming has generated immense reactions from all sides.

Fish farms began appearing in the late 1970s; in 2012 there are 130 operations in BC. Located in protected inlets and bays, the farms provide millions of pounds of salmon to a growing middle class around the world that appreciates salmon's health benefits and delicious taste. Unaffected by weather and seas, migration cycles and predators, grown-to-order fish are available throughout the year.

After a moratorium on new fish farms from 1985 to 2002 in order to study their environmental impacts, fish farming has become the province's largest agricultural export, outstripping any other industry and projected to contribute a billion dollars to the province's GDP by 2020. Fish farmers insist this is the only way to take the pressure off the wild stocks and create a viable mass-produced food product.

With commercial fishing, sport fishing and salmon farming each bringing in approximately $300 to $350 million per year in the early 2000s, anti–fish farm protesters argue that employment figures are significantly higher for sport and commercial fishing, at nearly 4,000 jobs compared to approximately 1,500 jobs for fish farming, and without the attendant environmental risk. And that does not include nature-based tourism, of which salmon is a part, coming in at nearly $7 billion and over 120,000 jobs.

At the same time, other marine-related sectors and environmental agencies have voiced significant concern over such issues as contamination of wild stock as they swim by the farm cages, contamination of waters by concentrated fecal matter and uneaten food, use of other fish in the feed pellets, and escape of farmed Atlantic salmon into wild Pacific stock. The greatest concern is the impact on young smolts and fry that are too fragile to survive sea lice and disease.

And so the argument rages on.

Annual catches and fishers' incomes have roller coastered for the last 100 years. Following the devastating aftermath of the Hells Gate rockslide, annual catches slowly increased to a high point of

93,210 tons in 1936. A gradual decline followed, then numbers began to reverse again in the late 1970s, with annual salmon catches reaching historic high levels of 107,500 tons in 1985. From that peak, catches fell rapidly to a historic low of 17,000 tons in 1999, totals that bumped up only marginally in the early 2000s.

Since the late 1990s, severe restrictions have almost eliminated commercial coho fishing and seriously reduced spring salmon harvests to less than two percent of total catch. Restrictions have been based on an extraordinary decline in what used to be considered *junk fish* only a hundred years before, with the burden falling on commercial fishers. Numerous sources claim the extraordinary decline is due to increasingly unfavourable ocean conditions—mostly to do with rising temperatures and acid levels—resulting in far fewer salmon returning to spawn.

But humans are a resourceful species, hard-wired for ingenuity and survival. From this marine crisis comes new awareness and innovative approaches. Often in partnership, fishers, government and ecologists are searching for solutions, from barcoding to Frankenfish.

Concerned with mounting ecological issues and dramatically decreasing catches, a group of commercial ling cod and salmon troller fishers on Vancouver Island approached Ecotrust Canada to collaborate on a tracking system that would encourage sustainable fishing practices. In May 2010, Thisfish, the world's first consumer-focused seafood tracking system, was launched, bringing fishers, organizations, businesses and consumers together in an open communication system through bar codes and the Internet.

Designed to help consumers and businesses make more informed choices in support of sustainable fishing practices and quality seafood, Thisfish now includes several other BC fish and seafood species and the Atlantic lobster fishery, and there are plans for expansion to shellfish.

When the fish or seafood is caught, it's tagged and given a Thisfish.info code that is uploaded to a website where the fisher enters information about catch-date, gear-type, location and even the crew. Consumers don't just ensure the freshness of their dinner, they also have an opportunity to connect with the fishers, person-to-person.

Thisfish is also partnering with conservation groups who act as watchdogs for bad fishing practices. Similar to Monterey Bay Aquarium's Seafood Watch program that has a smartphone app to rate the ocean-friendliness of seafoods as *Best Choice, Good Alternative* or *Avoid*, Thisfish publishes the eco-ratings of Seafood Watch, the Marine Stewardship Council, SeaChoice and Ocean Wise, and links to government websites.

Currently almost 300 fishing vessels are tracking their catch at Thisfish.info and codes for over five million pounds of seafood have been uploaded. As of April 2012, 130 fishing vessels in the salmon, halibut, ling cod, sablefish, sockeye and prawn fisheries in BC have participated, with more than 125 Atlantic lobster vessels and nearly 150,000 lobsters traced. Coded products have been distributed to 540 cities in 23 countries around the world.

Studies in Canada and the United States also claim that commercial salmon-trolling practices have the lowest impacts on salmon stocks and the marine environment. Monterey Bay Aquarium's Seafood Watch has also identified trolling as an environmentally responsible fishing method. Non-targeted fish are quickly and easily removed from the barbless hooks. Selective gear also increases survival rate. The slow pace and personal handling of fish ensure the highest-quality salmon for the marketplace.

The Vancouver Aquarium Ocean Wise seafood conservation program educates and supports consumers to make sustainable, ocean-friendly buying decisions. From suppliers to markets to restaurants to educational institutions, Ocean Wise currently has over 450 members and partners in almost 3,000 locations. Over 90 fish and seafood types are identified on its website *oceanwise.ca* and rated for sustainability. Overfishing is cited as the greatest threat to marine ecology, with harvests doubling from the 1970s to approximately 130 million tonnes every year. Consumers are urged to purchase only seafood bearing the Ocean Wise logo, whether from menus or through distributors.

Ocean Wise also recommends purchasing seafood harvested by trolling and other forms of hook-and-line fishing because of the low impact to species and the marine environment. They agree that aquaculture can take pressure off wild stocks and provide viable protein but only if done with extreme care and judiciousness.

Fish and seafood farming, the fastest-growing food-production industry in the world, is under enormous pressure to improve its systems and environmental track record. The Integrated Multi-Trophic Aquaculture (IMTA) approach is slowly gaining momentum, particularly with the high-risk potential of salmon and other carnivorous fish raised in ocean pens. Functioning like a natural interrelated ecosystem, bottom feeders like urchins and lobsters eat the excess feed falling to the bottom, thereby reducing bacterial contamination. Cleaners such as mussels and other shellfish filter the excrement, decreasing pollution. Bottom-growing seaweed is fertilized by the dissolved waste created by the shellfish and then harvested for fish feed to complete the cycle.

The Nature Conservancy's Central Coast Groundfish Project is a leading-edge program that addresses the profound damage to the sea floor by bottom-scraping trawl nets. Working with commercial fishers, the project is developing more sustainable and environmentally responsible harvesting practices for groundfish like sole and rockfish. A unique system of buying back trawling licences returns money to the commercial fishers. They can either leave the industry or lease the licences at affordable fees with the proviso of meeting stringent conservation criteria. Along with revised harvesting methods that supply groundfish to a growing sustainability market, almost four million acres of no-trawl zones have been designated off the California coast.

But the biggest bogeyman in the modern dream of sustainability is transgenic technology—the genetically modified Frankenfish. Even though the number of genetically modified *plant*-based foods is increasing, as is the general public's concerns, scientists have been cautious about creating genetically modified *animals*. Despite growing concern for human health issues and the possibility of genetic mishaps escaping, destroying or competing with wild stocks, some experts suggest engineering specific existing animals into *higher sustainability*. Take the gene of the bigger spring salmon and splice it into the smaller Atlantic salmon, where the gene causes a growth hormone to make it grow faster and bigger. Some argue that humans have been altering animals through selective breeding for thousands of years, and gene alteration will just promote faster change. Soon a transgenic trout that can be raised in ponds or vats will be able to provide 10 to 20 percent more muscle tissue.

And some people believe that the harvesting of wild fish and the ways of its courageous independents will never die, but will transform, shift and change. Maybe become a high-end boutique venture, like truffles or cheese or ice wine, with the harvesters finally being paid what their wares are worth.

As the Northwest seas continue to warm and acidify, the water rises to reclaim the land wrestled from it so long ago; as the silent kelp beds fill the inlets and choke the harbours and shipping lanes while saving the air and water with their life-giving chemistry, the hunters will follow their quarry north, and north, and more north, to the dark Arctic waters of their Sisiutl.

The last bastion of the Fraser River salmon-canning industry, now a museum: Gulf of Georgia Cannery, at the government wharf in Steveston, on the Lower Mainland. PAUL TAYLOR

Dennis Davidson

Sylvia Taylor is an award-winning freelance writer, editor, educator, and communications specialist. With hundreds of magazine and newspaper articles in print, she has worked with numerous manuscripts through all stages of writing and publishing. Sylvia is a popular speaker, conference presenter and writing competition judge throughout North America. She lives in Metro Vancouver; visit her at sylviataylor.ca.